Name _____

I Can Taste

I have one tongue.

I can taste sweet red apples.

I taste salty popcorn.

My tongue helps to taste.

1. What tastes sweet?

_____

2. What tastes salty?

_____

3. What color are the apples?

_____

4. What helps you to taste?

_____

5. How many tongues do you have?

_____

     FS-32048 Science

I Can Feel

I have ten fingers.

I can feel a soft kitten.

I feel hard rocks and cold ice.

My fingers help me to feel.

1. What feels soft?

_____

_____

2. What feels hard?

_____

_____

3. What feels cold?

_____

_____

4. What helps you to feel?

_____

_____

5. How many fingers do you have?

_____

_____

Did You Know?

You can see with your eyes.
Ears hear and noses smell.
You have taste buds on your tongue.

Turtles have tongues!

1. With what do you hear?

_____

2. How do you see?

_____

3. With what do you smell?

_____

4. Where are your taste buds?

_____

*5. Name something you like to taste.

_____

11

Name _____

In the Garden
Many plants have flowers.
Flowers help make seeds.
Some flowers turn to face the sun.

1. What do many plants have?

_____

- -

_____

2. What do flowers help make?

_____

- -

_____

3. What can some flowers do?

_____

- -

_____

Draw some flowers for Jack. Color the picture.

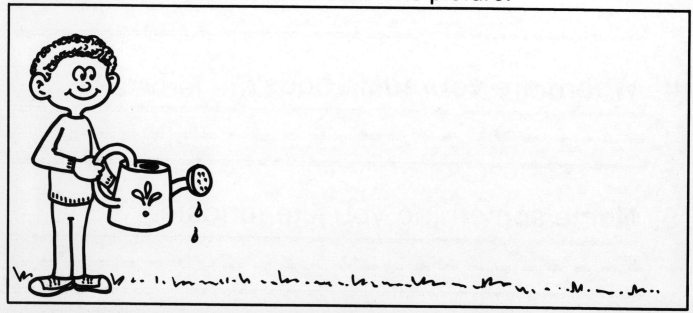

FS-32048 Science

Drip, Drip

Plants need water to grow.
The roots take up water from the soil.
The water goes up the stem to the leaves.

1. What do plants need?

_____

2. How does the water get into the plant?

_____

3. Where are the plant's roots?

_____

4. How does the water get to the leaves?

_____

*5. What else do you think plants need?

_____

Pet Care

A pet needs lots of love.
Feed it the kind of food that it needs.
Do you know that a pet can get sick
if it is bored?

1. What does a pet need?

2. What do we feed a pet?

3. What can happen to a bored pet?

*4. How can you find out what is the right food
for your pet?

*5. What can you do with a dog so that it will not
be bored?

FS-32048 Science

Exotic Pets

Gasp!

It is very hard to keep wild animals.
They may need a big space to run around.
They may eat food that is hard
to get—like live spiders!

1. What is hard to do well?

_____

2. What might wild animals need?

_____

3. What might they need to eat?

_____

*4. Do you have a zoo in your city?

_____

*5. What are some things that a zoo keeper
   will need to know?

_____

FS-32048 Science

Name _____

Sally Spider

A spider has eight legs.
A spider is not an insect.
Spiders eat insects!
Some spiders make webs.

1. How many legs do spiders have?

_____

- -

_____

2. What do some spiders make?

_____

- -

_____

3. What do spiders eat?

_____

- -

_____

Draw spiders on the web.

16

Who Made the Holes?

Did you ever look at rocks at the seashore?
Some of the stones have holes in them.
Some clams make holes in soft stones.

1. Where can you find rocks with holes?

_____

_____

2. What can make holes in stones?

_____

_____

3. What is another word for **rock**?

_____

_____

*4. Have you ever gone to the seashore?

_____

_____

*5. Why do you think a clam makes holes
   in stones?

_____

_____

FS-32048 Science

Time to Hibernate

In winter, some animals hide and become **dormant**. That means they are very still, as if they were asleep. My turtle stays in his hole from November to March!

1. When do some animals hide?

2. What does **dormant** mean?

3. When does my turtle hide in his hole?

*4. What word means hide for the winter?

*5. Why do you think some animals hibernate?

Name

Camouflage

Some animals use color to hide themselves.

A green bug is hard to see on a leaf.

Some rabbits turn white in winter
to match the snow.

1. How do some animals hide?

2. What is hard to see on a leaf?

3. What do some rabbits do in winter?

*4. What color is snow?

*5. Where do you think a brown lizard can hide?

FS-32048 Science

Nocturnal Animals

Some animals sleep in the daytime.
They come out at night to look for food.
Many desert animals like to come out at night.

1. What do some animals do in the daytime?

_ _

2. When do they come out?

_ _

3. What do they do at night?

_ _

4. What kind of animals like to come out
   at night?

_ _

*5. Why do many desert animals like to come
   out at night?

_ _

Newborns

Mama?

Some baby animals are born bald and blind.
They need their mothers for a long time.
Other babies are born with hair.
They are a lot like small adults.

1. Why do some babies need their mothers for a
   long time?

   _____

   _____

2. What are other babies like?

   _____

   _____

3. What are some babies born with?

   _____

   _____

*4. Find a word that means **can't see**.

   _____

   _____

*5. Find a word that means **has no hair**.

   _____

   _____

21

FS-32048 Science

Name _____

Wild Animals

Some animals in the woods look so cute.
You may want to take them home with you.
I hope you will leave them free and happy
in the woods.

1. How do some wild animals look?

_____

_____

2. What is it that you may want to do?

_____

_____

3. What do I hope you will do?

_____

_____

*4. What can happen if you pick up a
    wild animal?

_____

_____

*5. What wild animal looks cute to you?

_____

_____

Rolling in the Mud

Why do some animals roll in dust or mud?
Mud can keep away bugs that bite.
It can also protect skin from sunburn.

1. What do some animals roll in?

_____

_____

2. What can bite animals?

_____

_____

3. How can mud protect skin?

_____

_____

*4. How do **people** keep bugs away?

_____

_____

*5. How do you protect your skin from the sun?

_____

_____

All Gone

Some animals are extinct.
That means there are none of them left now.
It is sad when an animal is the last of its kind.

1. What has happened to some kinds of animals?

   _____

   _____

2. What does extinct mean?

   _____

   _____

3. What is sad?

   _____

   _____

*4. Do you think dinosaurs are extinct?

   _____

   _____

*5. Do you wish fleas were extinct?

   _____

   _____

Mammals

Mammals have fur or hair.
Mammals have milk for their babies.
A person is a mammal, and so is a bunny.

1. What do mammals have for their babies?

2. What else do mammals have?

3. Are you a mammal?

*4. Name a big mammal.

*5. Name a tiny mammal.

Name _____

Mammals in the Sea

Some mammals live in the sea.
A mother whale feeds milk to her baby.
Whales have to come up to breathe air.

1. Name a big sea mammal.

_____

_ _ _ _ _ _ _ _ _ _ _ _ _ _ _ _ _ _ _ _

2. What does a mother whale feed her baby?

_ _ _ _ _ _ _ _ _ _ _ _ _ _ _ _ _ _ _ _

3. Why do whales come up?

_____

_ _ _ _ _ _ _ _ _ _ _ _ _ _ _ _ _ _ _ _

*4. What kind of animal can breathe under water?

_____

_ _ _ _ _ _ _ _ _ _ _ _ _ _ _ _ _ _ _ _

*5. Do you think that a whale is a fish?

_____

_ _ _ _ _ _ _ _ _ _ _ _ _ _ _ _ _ _ _ _

FS-32048 Science

Rodents

Rodents are a kind of mammal.
Rats, mice and beavers are rodents.
They have teeth that can chew very well!

1. Are rodents a kind of mammal?

2. What can rodents do very well?

3. Name some rodents.

*4. Do you know someone who has a pet rodent?

*5. Name a rodent that can sometimes be a pest.

FS-32048 Science

Pass the Cheese!

Here is a mouse.
Mice are small mammals.
Farmers say mice are pests.
Some mice are pets.

1. Name one small mammal.

   _____

   -

   _____

2. What do farmers call mice?

   -

   _____

3. What are some mice?

   -

Draw some little gray mice.

28

FS-32048 Science

The Elephant

The elephant is big and gray.

His nose is a long trunk.

He eats leaves from tree tops.

1. What is big?

_____

2. What color is the elephant?

_____

3. What is long?

_____

4. What do elephants eat?

_____

5. Where are the leaves?

_____

FS-32048 Science

Name _____

Ellen Elephant

Elephants are large mammals.
Their big ears help keep them cool.
Their trunks are handy!

1. What are elephants?

   _____

   -

2. How do their big ears help them?

   _____

   -

3. What handy thing does an elephant have?

   _____

   -

Draw an elephant to eat the peanuts.

FS-32048 Science

Cats

Cats have four soft paws.
Cats keep their claws sharp.
They like to climb tall trees.

1. What are soft?

_____

_____

2. What are sharp?

_____

_____

3. What can cats climb?

_____

_____

4. How many paws do cats have?

_____

_____

5. What are tall?

_____

_____

FS-32048 Science

Here, Kitty!

A lion is a big cat.
Some cats are pets.
Cats eat meat and fish.
Some cats hunt for mice.

1. What do cats eat?

_____

- -

_____

2. Name one very big cat.

- -

_____

3. What are some cats?

_____

- -

_____

Draw a cat. Color it yellow.

FS-32048 Science

Wally Walrus

This walrus is fat.
Fat keeps him warm.
He swims in cold water.

1. What is Wally?

   _____

   -

   _____

2. Where does Wally swim?

   _____

   -

   _____

3. What does fat do for Wally?

   _____

   -

   _____

Draw a walrus on the ice.

FS-32048 Science

Sniff, Sniff

Bears like to eat.
They can smell very well.
Do not keep food in your tent.
A bear might visit you.

1. What do bears like to do?

   _____

   -

   _____

2. What do bears do very well?

   -

   _____

3. What should not be in your tent?

   _____

   -

   _____

Draw a big brown bear.

FS-32048 Science

Baa, Baa

This is a mammal.
It is a sheep.
The sheep's fur gives us wool.
A lamb is a baby sheep.

1. What do you call a baby sheep?

----

2. What do we get from sheep?

----

3. Are sheep mammals?

Draw a furry sheep here.

Bunny Rabbits

Rabbits are also called bunnies.
A bunny has soft fur.
A bunny is a mammal.
Bunnies eat plants.

1. What do bunnies have?

_____

2. What do bunnies eat?

_____

3. What else can you call a bunny?

_____

Draw a happy bunny by the carrot.

Name _____

Flap, Flap!

Bats can fly.
Bats are not birds.
Bats are like flying mice.
Some bats eat fruit.

1. What can bats do?

_____

- -

_____

2. Are bats birds?

_____

- -

_____

3. What are bats like?

_____

- -

_____

Draw a bat in the night sky.

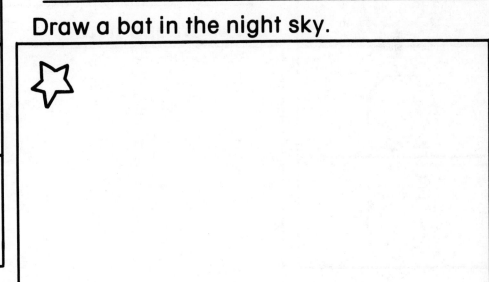

FS-32048 Science

Name _____

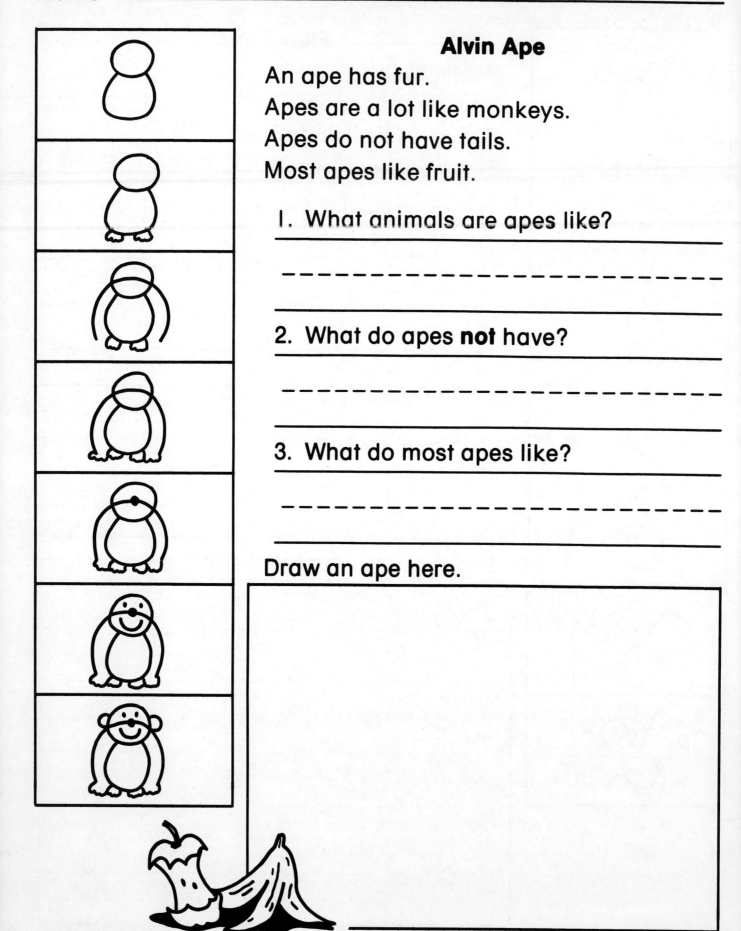

Alvin Ape

An ape has fur.

Apes are a lot like monkeys.

Apes do not have tails.

Most apes like fruit.

1. What animals are apes like?

_____

- -

_____

2. What do apes **not** have?

_____

- -

_____

3. What do most apes like?

_____

- -

_____

Draw an ape here.

38

Marsupials

Some animals keep their babies in a pouch. At first, the babies stay in there all the time. Later they go in and out.

1. Where do some animals keep their babies?

2. What do the babies do at first?

3. Later what do the babies do?

*4. Name an animal with a pouch.

*5. Do you think that a pouch is handy? Why?

Name _____

Kangaroos

The gray kangaroo can hop fast.

She has strong back legs.

The baby is in her soft pocket.

1. What can hop fast?

_____

_____

2. What are strong?

_____

_____

3. What is soft?

_____

_____

4. Where is the baby?

_____

_____

5. What color is the kangaroo?

_____

_____

FS-32048 Science

Reptiles

A reptile has dry skin with scales.
A snake is one kind of reptile.
Dinosaurs were reptiles.

1. What kind of skin do reptiles have?

_____

_____

2. Name one kind of reptile.

_____

_____

3. Name a big reptile of long ago.

_____

_____

*4. Name another reptile.

_____

_____

*5. Do you think snakes feel wet and slimy?

_____

_____

Other Eggs

The little egg will soon hatch.
No bird will come out of it.
This egg is a turtle egg!

1. Is the egg big or little?

_____

_____

2. What will the egg soon do?

_____

_____

3. Will a bird come out?

_____

_____

4. Did a bird lay this egg?

_____

_____

*5. What **will** come out?

_____

_____

FS-32048 Science

Timmy Turtle

This turtle lives on land.
It does not have fur.
It has a hard shell.
Some turtles live in the water.

1. Where does this turtle live?

_____

_____

2. Where do some turtles live?

_____

_____

3. What does this turtle have?

_____

_____

Draw a land turtle. Color the picture.

43

FS-32048 Science

Baby Lizards

Mama ?

Some lizards are born alive.
Other kinds of lizards lay eggs.
Baby lizards are in those eggs.

1. Do all lizards lay eggs?

2. Do some lizards lay eggs?

*3. What other kinds of animals lay eggs?

4. What comes out of a lizard egg?

*5. Have you ever seen a bird egg?

44

The Alligator

The alligator lives near water.

He has a long brown tail.

The tail helps him to swim.

He likes to eat fish.

1. Where does the alligator live?

   _____

   _____

2. What is long?

   _____

   _____

3. What color is his tail?

   _____

   _____

4. How does his tail help him?

   _____

   _____

5. What does he like to eat?

   _____

   _____

FS-32048 Science

Amphibians

Some animals are born in water.
At first, they live under water like a fish.
Then they grow legs and lungs,
and live out on land!

1. Where are amphibians born?

_____

_____

2. What are they like at first?

_____

_____

3. Then what do they grow?

_____

_____

4. Then where do they live?

_____

_____

*5. Have you ever seen a real live frog or toad?

_____

_____

The Tadpole

The tadpole came from an egg.
Then it grew tiny legs.
The tadpole became a frog!

1. What came from the egg?

_ _

2. What grew on the tadpole?

_ _

3. What will the tadpole become?

_ _

*4. What do frogs eat?

_ _

*5. Guess where you can look for tadpoles and frogs.

_ _

Name _____

Big frogs hop around.
Baby frogs are tadpoles.
Tadpoles live in water.

1. How do big frogs get around?

   -

2. Where do baby frogs live?

   -

3. What do you call baby frogs?

   -

Make some frogs on the log.

Name _____

Is It a Bird?

Birds have feathers.
Most birds can fly.
Some birds eat seeds.

1. What do birds have?

_____

- -

_____

2. What can most birds do?

_____

- -

_____

3. What do some birds eat?

_____

- -

_____

Draw two birds. Color the picture.

Birds

A bird has a beak and two legs.
Some birds can fly.
Bird eggs have hard shells.

1. What do birds have?

   _____

   _ _ _ _ _ _ _ _ _ _ _ _ _ _ _ _ _

2. What can some birds do?

   _____

   _ _ _ _ _ _ _ _ _ _ _ _ _ _ _ _ _

3. What has a hard shell?

   _____

   _ _ _ _ _ _ _ _ _ _ _ _ _ _ _ _ _

4. How many legs do birds have?

   _____

   _ _ _ _ _ _ _ _ _ _ _ _ _ _ _ _ _

*5. Is a butterfly a kind of bird?

   _____

   _ _ _ _ _ _ _ _ _ _ _ _ _ _ _ _ _

Nesting Time

Some birds make a nest to hold their eggs.
Other birds lay their eggs right on the ground!
These eggs often look like rocks.
This helps to hide them.

1. What do some birds make?

_____

_____

2. Where do other birds lay their eggs?

_____

_____

3. What do these eggs often look like?

_____

_____

*4. Why do birds want to hide their eggs?

_____

_____

*5. What do birds use to make nests?

_____

_____

FS-32048 Science

Some Birds Migrate

Some birds stay with us
even in the cold wintertime.
They have to look hard to find food.
Other birds fly away to lands that are warm.

1. Do some birds stay with us in winter?

_____

_____

2. What do other birds do?

_____

_____

3. Why do some birds fly away?

_____

_____

*4. Why is it hard to find food in winter?

_____

_____

*5. Name some things that birds eat.

_____

_____

FS-32048 Science

Robins

The mother robin makes the nest.

The nest is in a big tree.

Five blue eggs are in the nest.

1. Who makes the nest?

_____

_____

2. Where is the nest?

_____

_____

3. How many eggs are in the nest?

_____

_____

4. What color are the eggs?

_____

_____

5. Can the mother robin fly?

_____

_____

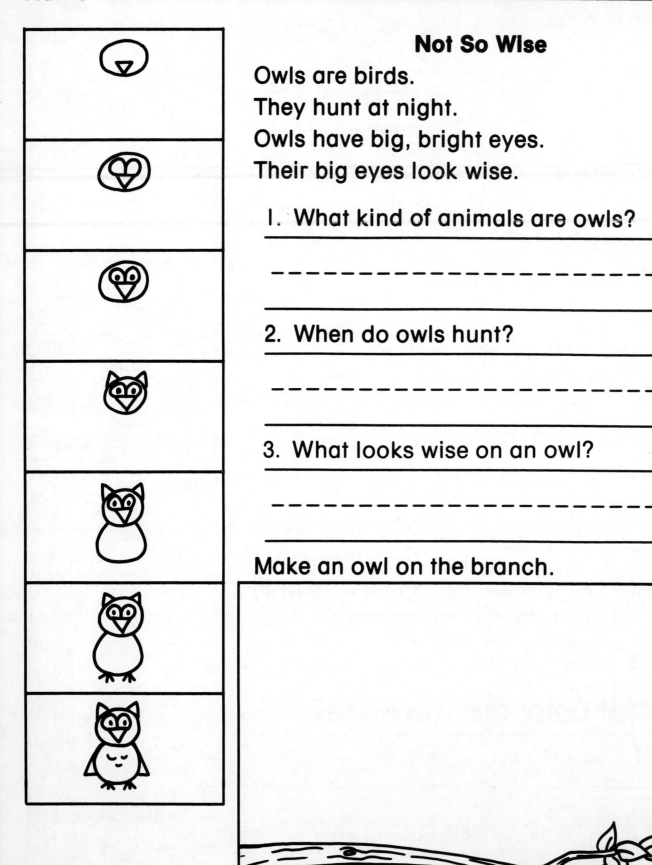

Not So Wise

Owls are birds.
They hunt at night.
Owls have big, bright eyes.
Their big eyes look wise.

1. What kind of animals are owls?

_____

_____

2. When do owls hunt?

_____

_____

3. What looks wise on an owl?

_____

_____

Make an owl on the branch.

54

FS-32048 Science

Name _____

Polly Penguin

Penguins are birds.
Penguins do not fly.
They are good swimmers.

1. What is Polly?

_____

- -

_____

2. What do penguins do well?

_____

- -

_____

3. What is it that penguins can't do?

_____

- -

_____

Draw some penguin friends for Polly.

FS-32048 Science

Fish

Fish have scales.
They can breathe under water.
Some fish live in salt water.

1. What do fish have?

_____

2. Where can fish breathe?

_____

3. Where do some fish live?

_____

*4. Do fish have fur?

_____

*5. Do fish have legs?

_____

FS-32048 Science

Name _____

In the Pond

Fish live in water.
Fish have scales.
Some fish eat bugs.

1. Where do fish live?

_____

- - - - - - - - - - - - - - - - - - - -

_____

2. What do fish have?

_____

- - - - - - - - - - - - - - - - - - - -

_____

3. What do some fish eat?

_____

- - - - - - - - - - - - - - - - - - - -

_____

Draw some fish in the water.

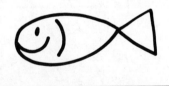

FS-32048 Science

Name _____

Insects

An insect has six legs.

Most insects have wings.

A butterfly is a pretty insect.

1. How many legs do insects have?

_____

_____

2. Do most insects have wings?

_____

_____

3. What is pretty?

_____

_____

4. Is a butterfly an insect?

_____

_____

5. How many legs does a butterfly have?

_____

_____

58

Name _____

Grasshoppers

Grasshoppers can jump far.
They eat green leaves in fields.
Some birds eat grasshoppers.

1. What can jump far?

_____

_____

2. What do grasshoppers eat?

_____

_____

3. What color are the leaves?

_____

_____

4. What do some birds eat?

_____

_____

5. Where are the green leaves?

_____

_____

FS-32048 Science

Name _____

Honeybees

Honeybees are helpful insects.

They make sweet honey and wax.

Bees help flowers become fruit.

1. Which insects are helpful?

_____

_____

2. What is sweet?

_____

_____

3. What makes wax?

_____

_____

4. What do flowers become?

_____

_____

5. Are honeybees insects?

_____

_____

Crickets

A cricket is a jumping insect.
Some crickets go into houses.
Crickets rub their wings to sing.

1. What is a cricket?

_____

_____

2. Where do some crickets go?

_____

_____

3. How do crickets sing?

_____

_____

4. Do crickets jump?

_____

_____

5. Could you have a cricket in your house?

_____

_____

 FS-32048 Science

Betty Beetle

Betty is an insect.
Insects have six legs.
Some insects eat plants.

1. What is Betty Beetle?

_____

- -

_____

2. What do some insects eat?

_____

- -

_____

3. How many legs do insects have?

_____

- -

_____

Draw some beetles on this plant.

Caterpillars

Caterpillars are baby butterflies.
The caterpillars eat plants.
They make a cocoon.
Then the adult butterfly comes out!

1. What are baby butterflies?

_____

_____

2. What do they eat?

_____

_____

3. What do they make?

_____

_____

Draw a butterfly. Color the picture.

Before Butterflies

A tiny egg lay on a leaf.
Out came a caterpillar!
It ate lots of leaves.

1. Where was the egg?

_____

_____

2. Was the egg big or tiny?

_____

_____

3. What came out of the egg?

_____

_____

4. What did the caterpillar eat?

_____

_____

*5. Guess what the caterpillar will become.

_____

_____

Surprise

The caterpillar turned into a pupa.
It lay very still for many weeks.
Then out came a butterfly.

1. What turned into a pupa?

   _____

2. Did the pupa move around?

   _____

3. How long did it lie still?

   _____

4. What came out of the pupa?

   _____

*5. Have you ever seen a caterpillar?

   _____

Name

The Moth

Some caterpillars do not become butterflies.
Many of them become moths.
A moth is a lot like a butterfly.

1. Do all caterpillars become butterflies?

2. What is like a butterfly?

3. Name two things a caterpillar may become.

*4. Were you once a caterpillar?

*5. How is a moth like a butterfly?

FS-32048 Science

Pests

Many caterpillars are **pests**.
They will eat buds and leaves.
They may make holes in your fruit!

1. What do we call caterpillars who are a bother?

   _____

   _____

2. What will they eat?

   _____

   _____

3. What do they do to fruit?

   _____

   _____

*4. Can you name another pest?

   _____

   _____

*5. What do you think **pest** means?

   _____

   _____

Inside an Apple

You may find a caterpillar in your apple.
Most people will call it a worm.
A caterpillar is a little like a worm.

1. Where can you find a caterpillar?

_____

_____

2. What will some people call it?

_____

_____

3. What is like a caterpillar?

_____

_____

*4. How are caterpillars and worms alike?

_____

_____

*5. Did you ever find a bug in your food?

_____

_____

Will It Float?

Fill a pail with water.
Drop little things in the water.
Make a chart to show what floats.

1. Where will you put the water? ....

   _____

2. What goes into the water?

   _____

3. Then what will you make?

   _____

4. What will it show?

   _____

*5. Name something you think will sink.

   _____

FS-32048 Science

Like Magic

Your teacher may have a magnet.
A magnet will not stick to wood or paper.
It will stick to some kinds of metal.

1. Who may have a magnet?

_____

_____

2. What does not stick to a magnet?

_____

_____

3. What may stick to a magnet?

_____

_____

*4. Is there a magnet in your class?

_____

_____

*5. Name some little things you think will stick
   to a magnet.

_____

_____

When You Play . . .

It is a good idea to have a friend with you.
If you get hurt, your pal can get help.
You are safer if you are not alone.

1. What is a good idea?

_____

_____

2. What can your pal do?

_____

_____

3. When can your pal get help?

_____

_____

4. When are you safer?

_____

_____

*5. Name a pal you like to play with.

_____

FS-32048 Science

Eat Healthy Foods

You need to eat good food each day.
Some good foods are milk, meat and fruit.
Don't eat too much junk food!

1. What do you need to eat each day?

   _

2. Name some good foods.

   _

*3. Name a fruit you like.

   _

*4. Name some junk foods.

   _

*5. How does good food help you?

   _

Clean Hands

Wash your hands before you eat.
Did you know little germs live there?
They are tiny, but they are real!

1. When should you wash your hands?

_ _

2. What may be on your hands?

_ _

3. What are tiny?

_ _

4. Are germs real?

_ _

*5. Why do we want to wash germs off?

_ _

Don't Sneeze on Me!

Cover your sneeze.
You can turn away, too.
Nobody wants to get your germs.

1. What do you cover?

   _____

   _____

2. What else can you do?

   _____

   _____

3. What is it nobody wants to get?

   _____

   _____

*4. Why not?

   _____

   _____

*5. Did you ever have a cold?

   _____

   _____

Taking Medicine

If you're sick, Mom may give you a pill.
Do not take a pill unless Mom
or Dad gives it to you.
You can become very sick if you do!

1. What can make you very sick?

2. When might Mom give you a pill?

*3. Should you give yourself pills?

*4. Do you take pills from other kids?

*5. Did you ever feel sick?

Be Kind to Animals

Do not tease any pets.
They have feelings, too!
Pets may scratch or bite if you scare them.

1. What do we never do to pets?

_____

_____

2. Why is it mean to tease pets?

_____

_____

3. What might scared pets do to you?

_____

_____

*4. What kind of pet do you like?

_____

_____

*5. Do you like people to tease you?

_____

_____

FS-32048 Science

Clean Up!

Put your toys away after you play.
Toys on the floor can trip people.
You may lose toys if you don't put them away.

1. What do you do after you play with toys?

_____

_____

2. What can trip people?

_____

_____

3. What can happen to toys if you don't put them away?

_____

_____

*4. Where do you keep your toys?

_____

_____

*5. Did you ever lose a toy?

_____

_____

Name _____

In the Car

Lovely!

Do not bother Mom when she is driving.
Stay in your seat belt and face the front.
If you fight or yell, Mom may crash!

1. Where do you stay when Mom is driving?

_____

_____

2. Where do you face?

_____

_____

3. If you fight, what may happen?

_____

_____

*4. Can Mom look at you and drive too?

_____

_____

*5. Can you put on your own seat belt?

_____

_____

78

Cross Carefully

Look both ways before you cross the street.
Try to cross at a corner or in a crosswalk.
If there is a light, wait for the green light.

1. How do you look before crossing?

_____

_____

2. Where do you try to cross?

_____

_____

3. What color light means go?

_____

_____

*4. What color light means stop?

_____

_____

*5. What does the yellow light mean?

_____

_____

Telephone Safety

Do you know how to use the telephone?
The telephone is not a toy.
Have someone show you how to
call for help.

1. Is the telephone a toy?

_ _

*2. Who can show you how to call on the telephone?

_ _

*3. What is your telephone number?

_ _

*4. What number can you call for help?

_ _

*5. Does your telephone have a dial, or buttons?

_ _

Happy Teeth

Try to brush your teeth each day.
Clean teeth look nice.
They will last a long, long time.

1. What do you need to do each day?

2. What looks nice?

3. What will clean teeth do?

*4. What color is your toothbrush?

*5. How can you take care of your teeth?

Look Out!

It is fun to run around.

But don't run in the kitchen by the stove.

Hot food can spill and burn you.

Slow down!

1. What is fun to do?

_____

_____

2. Where should you not run around?

_____

_____

3. Why not?

_____

_____

4. What may be hot in the kitchen?

_____

_____

*5. Name a place where it is all right to run around.

_____

_____

FS-32048 Science

Fire Safety

The smoke from a fire can make you very sick.
The good air is down by the floor.
Crawl to a safe place.

1. What can make you sick?

   _____

   _____

2. Where is the good air?

   _____

   _____

*3. Have you had a fire drill at school?

   _____

   _____

*4. Did you ever see a fire truck?

   _____

   _____

Fire Drill

How will you get out of the house
if there's a fire?
One way is to go out the front door!
You will need to know another way, too.

1. When might you need to get out of the
   house?

   _

2. Name one way to get out.

   _

3. What else do you need to know?

   _

*4. Why do you need to know two ways?

   _

*5. Does your room have a window?

   _

My Skeleton

There are many things inside of me that I cannot see. Some things I can feel.
Feel my head. Feel my fingers. Feel my knees. They are hard. They are bones. Bones make up my skeleton. There is a skeleton inside me!

1. How do bones feel?

_____

_____

2. What do bones make up?

_____

_____

Cut along this line.

FS-32048 Science

Paste other half of body here.

My skeleton gives me my shape. If I had no bones, I would be like a rag doll!

My bones protect the soft parts inside of me. My skull protects my brain. My ribs protect my lungs and heart.

1. What does my skeleton give me?

_____

_ _ _ _ _ _ _ _ _ _ _ _ _ _ _

_____

2. What kind of parts does it protect?

_____

_ _ _ _ _ _ _ _ _ _ _ _ _ _ _

_____

Color and cut out the parts on pages 87 and 88. Paste them on the body.

FS-32048 Science

Can you find these bones?

pelvis
skull
spine
collarbone
ribs

Find these bones on your body.

1.

2.

3.

4.

5.

CUT

CUT

CUT

CUT

CUT

CUT

CUT

CUT

Cut out the skeleton parts. Paste them on the body.

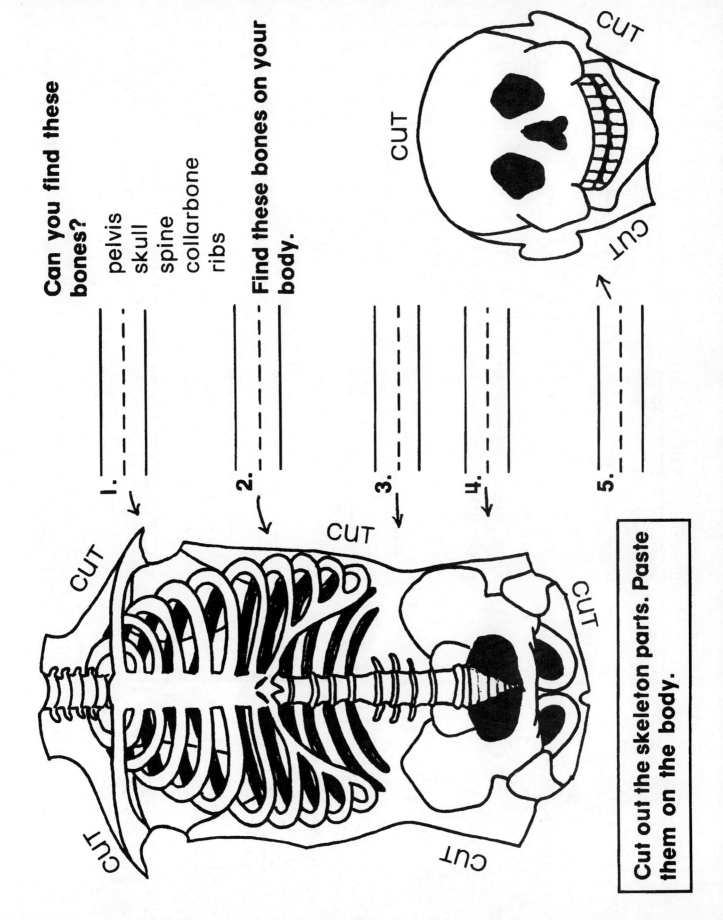

FS-32048 Science

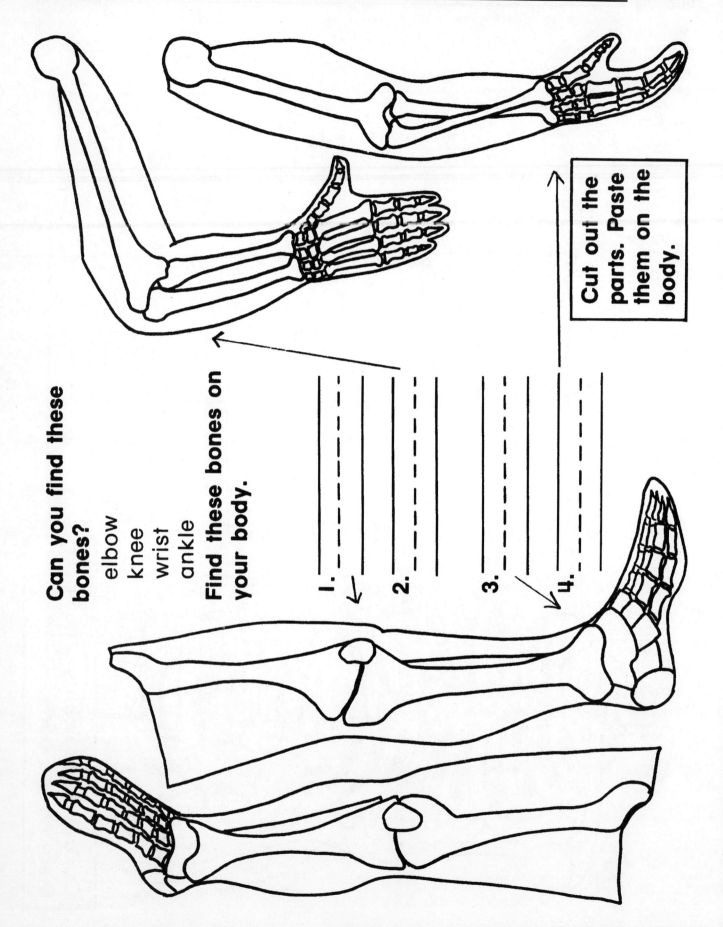

Can you find these bones?

elbow
knee
wrist
ankle

Find these bones on your body.

Cut out the parts. Paste them on the body.

1.
2.
3.
4.

88

My Muscles

My skeleton cannot move. It needs help. Muscles are the helpers. They move my bones. They move my bones! Muscles move me. Muscles move by pulling. They pull my bones.

1. What moves me?

_____

_____

2. How do they move me?

_____

_____

Cut along this line.

89

Name

Name _____

Paste other half of body here.

Some muscles pull my leg up.
Other muscles pull my leg down.
Muscles cannot push.
I need to run and play hard. This
makes my muscles strong.

1. What can't muscles do?

_____

_____

2. Why should I play hard?

_____

_____

**Color the muscles
red. Trace the dark
lines with a black
crayon.**

Eating

Cars need gas to run. I need food to live.

I put food in my mouth. I chew. I swallow. The food goes to my stomach. My stomach is made of muscle. It mixes up the food.

1. What is my stomach?

_____

_____

2. What does my stomach do?

_____

_____

Paste edge of "door" here.

Cut along this line.

FS-32048 Science

Paste other half of body here.

The food becomes soupy. It goes into a small tube. Then it goes into my blood. My blood takes it to all parts of my body.

The waste goes into a large tube. Then it leaves my body.

1. What takes the food to all parts of my body?

_ _ _ _ _ _ _ _ _ _ _ _ _ _ _

_ _ _ _ _ _ _ _ _ _ _ _ _ _ _

2. What goes into the large tube?

_ _ _ _ _ _ _ _ _ _ _ _ _ _ _

_ _ _ _ _ _ _ _ _ _ _ _ _ _ _

Color the boy as directed on page 93. Paste the "door" on.

FS-32048 Science

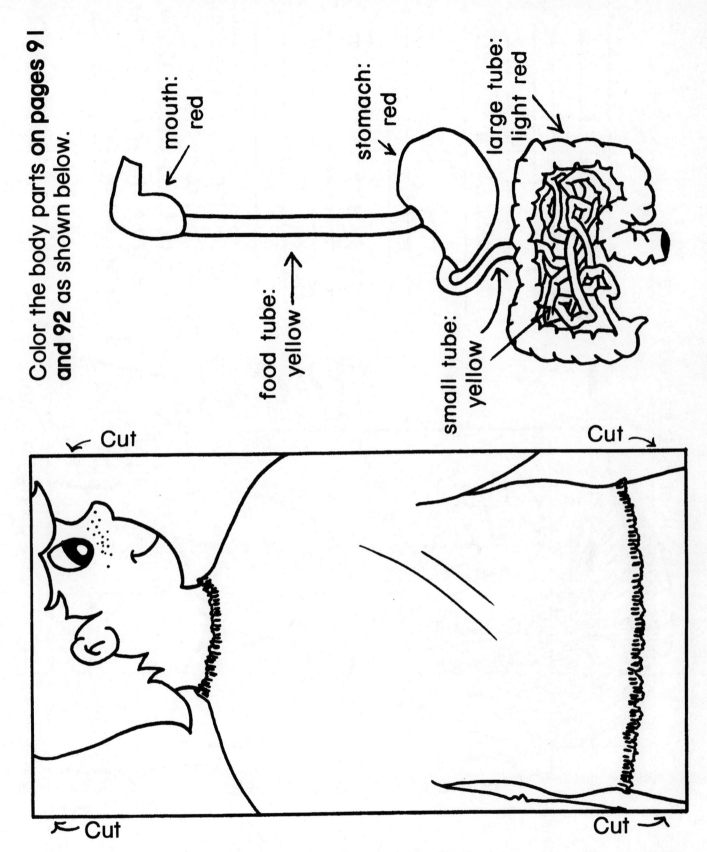

Color the body parts on pages 91 and 92 as shown below.

mouth: red

food tube: yellow

stomach: red

large tube: light red

small tube: yellow

Cut

Cut

Cut

Cut

Color the boy and cut out the "door." Paste it on pages 91 and 92.

FS-32048 Science

My Lungs

nostril

mouth

windpipe

lungs

heart

Color the girl as directed on page 96. Paste the "door" on. Trace the words. Draw lines from the words to the correct body parts.

Paste edge of "door" here.

Cut along this line.

FS-32048 Science

Paste page 94 here.

Breathing

I can live for weeks without food. I can live for days without water. I can live for only a few minutes without air.

Air goes through my nose or mouth. It goes down my windpipe. It goes into my lungs.

My lungs are like balloons. I fill them with air when I breathe. Then the air goes into my blood. My blood takes it to all parts of my body.

1. How long can you live without air?

_ _ _ _ _ _ _ _ _ _ _ _ _ _

_ _ _ _ _ _ _ _ _ _ _ _ _ _

2. What is the "air tube" called?

_ _ _ _ _ _ _ _ _ _ _ _ _ _

_ _ _ _ _ _ _ _ _ _ _ _ _ _

3. What are my lungs like?

_ _ _ _ _ _ _ _ _ _ _ _ _ _

_ _ _ _ _ _ _ _ _ _ _ _ _ _

4. How does air get to all parts of my body?

_ _ _ _ _ _ _ _ _ _ _ _ _ _

_ _ _ _ _ _ _ _ _ _ _ _ _ _

Color the body parts **on page 94.**

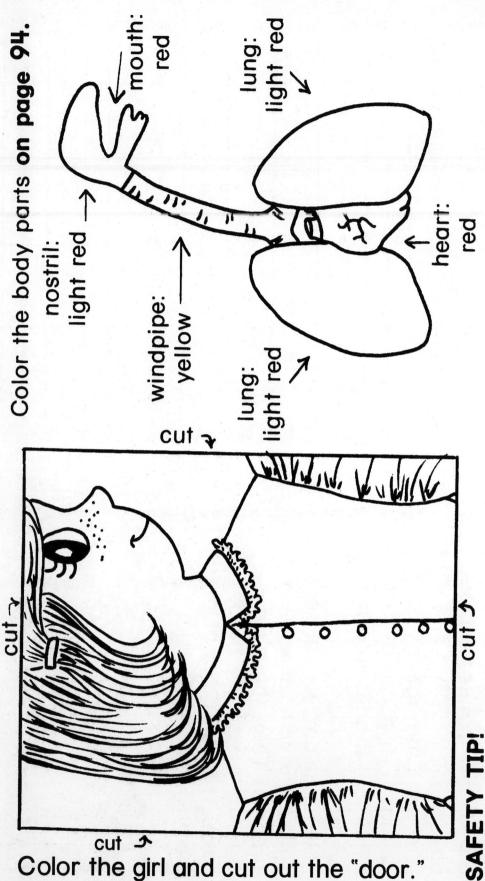

mouth:
red

lung:
light red

nostril:
light red

heart:
red

windpipe:
yellow

lung:
light red

cut ↗

cut ↗

cut ↗

cut ↗

Color the girl and cut out the "door."
Paste it on page **94**.

SAFETY TIP!

The windpipe has a little door over it. This is to make sure that
when you swallow, food will not go into the windpipe.
Sometimes you gulp air when you eat. Then the door opens.
Food goes in and and you choke. Someone must squeeze you
hard and fast just below your ribs. This makes air come up.
The door opens and out pops the food!

96

My Blood

My body needs food. My body needs air. Every part needs both food and air. How does food go from my stomach to my ear? How does air go from my lungs to my toes? My blood takes them!

1. What does my body need?

_____

_____

2. What takes them?

_____

_____

lungs

heart

Cut along this line.

FS-32048 Science

Paste other half of body here.

My body has miles of roads in it. These roads are long tubes. Blood flows through them. I must have blood! It keeps all of my body alive!

1. What are my roads?

_____

_ _ _ _ _ _ _ _ _

2. What does blood keep alive?

_____

_ _ _ _ _ _ _ _ _

Look at your skin. Can you find some tubes of blood? Color the blood in this body red.

FS-32048 Science

My Heart

Blood flows all through my body. What makes it move? My heart! My heart is made of muscle. It is a very strong pump. My blood moves because it is being pushed by my heart.

My heart is the size of my fist. It has four "rooms." It has two pumps. No one can live without a heart.

1. What moves my blood?

_____

_____

2. Of what is my heart made?

_____

_____

3. How big is my heart?

_____

_____

4. How many "rooms" does it have?

_____

_____

I have one, too!

START

from upper body

to upper body

Cut along this line.

FS-32048 Science

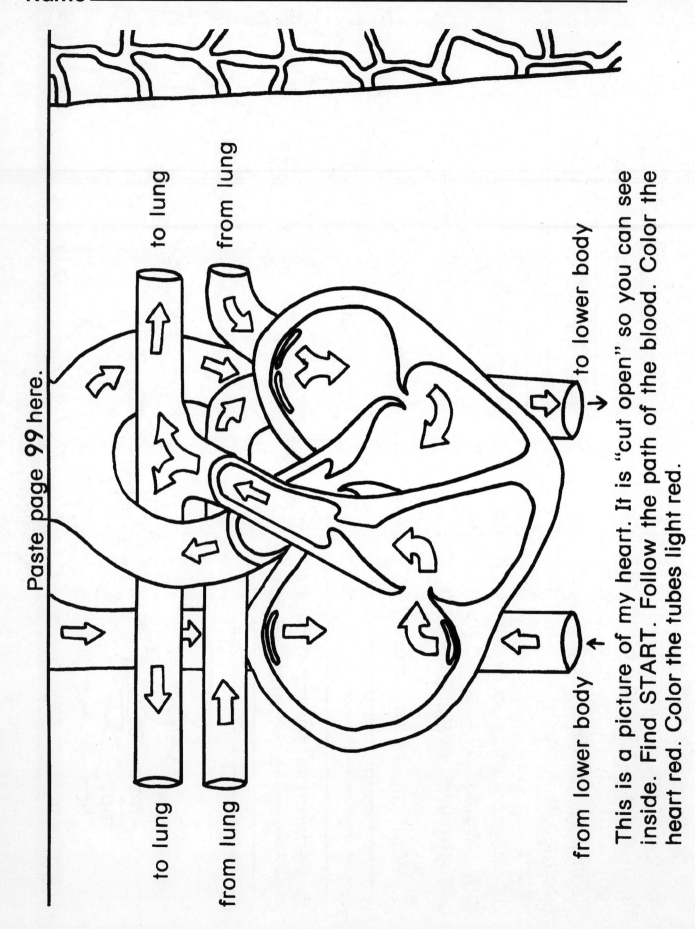

Paste page 99 here.

to lung

from lung

to lung

from lung

to lower body

from lower body

This is a picture of my heart. It is "cut open" so you can see inside. Find START. Follow the path of the blood. Color the heart red. Color the tubes light red.

FS-32048 Science

My Brain and Nerves

I could not live without my brain. It is the most important part of me. It makes my whole body work.

My brain tells my nerves what to do. My nerves go down my spine. They go to each part of my body. They tell each part what to do.

1. What keeps me alive?

_____

2. What helps my brain?

_____

Cut along this line.

101

Paste other half of body here.

My brain has three parts. One part keeps my body alive. One part helps me move. But the biggest part makes me think!

1. How many parts are in my brain?

_____

2. Where do I think?

_____

_____

Outline the body with a black crayon. Color the brain light red. Trace over the nerves in red.

FS-32048 Science

My Skin

I cannot see my bones. I cannot see my heart. I cannot see my muscles or my lungs. My skin covers all these parts. My skin protects me. My skin is alive. It grows as I grow.

1. What covers me?

_____

_ _ _ _ _ _ _ _ _ _ _ _ _ _ _

2. What happens to my skin when I grow?

_____

_ _ _ _ _ _ _ _ _ _ _ _ _ _ _

Cut along this line.

Paste other half of body here.

My skin protects me. It keeps germs out. My body is wet inside. My skin keeps me from drying out. When I get hot, my skin sweats. This cools me off.

Skin is great! All of me is super! I am glad I have a wonderful body!

1. What does skin keep out?

_____

- - - - - - - - - - - - - - - - -

_____

2. How does skin cool me?

_____

- - - - - - - - - - - - - - - - -

_____

This body is ME! I can color it to look like me. I'll cut out hair and clothes. I'll paste them on.

104

Answer Key

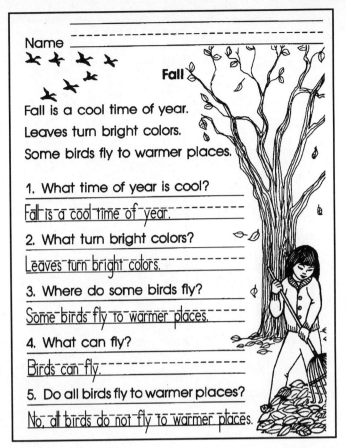

Name _____

Fall

Fall is a cool time of year.
Leaves turn bright colors.
Some birds fly to warmer places.

1. What time of year is cool?

Fall is a cool time of year.

2. What turn bright colors?

Leaves turn bright colors.

3. Where do some birds fly?

Some birds fly to warmer places.

4. What can fly?

Birds can fly.

5. Do all birds fly to warmer places?

No, all birds do not fly to warmer places.

Page 1

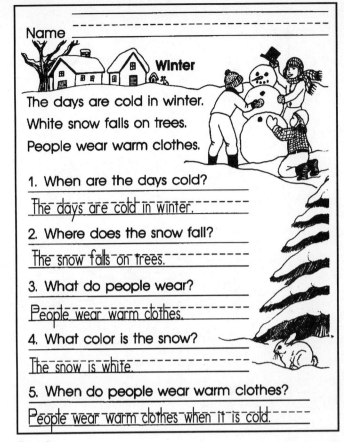

Name _____

Winter

The days are cold in winter.
White snow falls on trees.
People wear warm clothes.

1. When are the days cold?

The days are cold in winter.

2. Where does the snow fall?

The snow falls on trees.

3. What do people wear?

People wear warm clothes.

4. What color is the snow?

The snow is white.

5. When do people wear warm clothes?

People wear warm clothes when it is cold.

Page 2

Name _____

Snowflakes

Icy snowflakes are beautiful.
Most snowflakes have six sides.
No two snowflakes are alike.

1. What are beautiful?

Snowflakes are beautiful.

2. What are icy?

Snowflakes are icy.

3. Are snowflakes ever alike?

No, snowflakes are not ever alike.

4. Do most snowflakes have eight sides?

No, most snowflakes do not have eight sides.

5. How many sides do most snowflakes have?

Most snowflakes have six sides.

Page 3

Name _____

Spring

The air feels warm in the spring.
Plants begin to grow again.
Birds make nests for their babies.

1. When does the air feel warm?

The air feels warm in the spring.

2. What begins to grow again?

Plants begin to grow again.

3. Why do birds make nests?

Birds make nests for their babies.

4. Can you hear birds in the spring?

Yes, I can hear birds in the spring.

5. Can you see new green leaves in spring?

Yes, I can see new green leaves in spring.

Page 4

Answer Key

Summer

The sun is very hot in summer.
The flowers are very pretty.
Happy children play outdoors.

1. What is very hot?
The sun is very hot.

2. What are very pretty?
The flowers are very pretty.

3. When is the sun very hot?
The sun is very hot in summer.

4. Where do the children play?
The children play outdoors.

5. How do the children feel?
The children feel happy.

Page 5

Name

I Can See

I have two eyes.
I can see the blue sky.
I see three yellow birds.
My eyes help me to read.

1. What is blue?
The sky is blue.

2. What color are the birds?
The birds are yellow.

3. What helps you to read?
My eyes help me to read.

4. How many birds do you see?
I see three birds.

5. How many eyes do you have?
I have two eyes.

Page 6

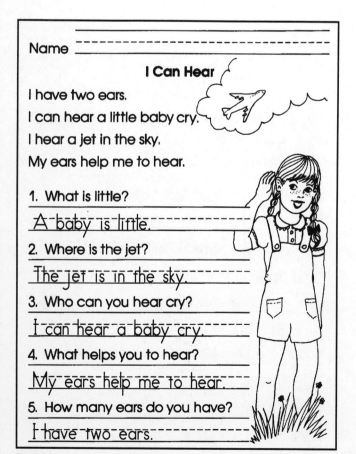

Name

I Can Hear

I have two ears.
I can hear a little baby cry.
I hear a jet in the sky.
My ears help me to hear.

1. What is little?
A baby is little.

2. Where is the jet?
The jet is in the sky.

3. Who can you hear cry?
I can hear a baby cry.

4. What helps you to hear?
My ears help me to hear.

5. How many ears do you have?
I have two ears.

Page 7

Name

I Can Smell

I have one nose.
I can smell the red rose.
I smell a hot apple pie.
My nose helps me to smell.

1. What is red?
The rose is red.

2. What is hot?
The pie is hot.

3. What is made of apples?
The pie is made of apples.

4. What helps you to smell?
My nose helps me to smell.

5. How many noses do you have?
I have one nose.

Page 8

106

FS-32048 Science

Answer Key

Name

I Can Taste

I have one tongue.
I can taste sweet red apples.
I taste salty popcorn.
My tongue helps to taste.

1. What tastes sweet?

   Red apples taste sweet.

2. What tastes salty?

   Popcorn tastes salty.

3. What color are the apples?

   The apples are red.

4. What helps you to taste?

   My tongue helps me to taste.

5. How many tongues do you have?

   I have one tongue.

Page 9

Name

I Can Feel

I have ten fingers.
I can feel a soft kitten.
I feel hard rocks and cold ice.
My fingers help me to feel.

1. What feels soft?

   A kitten feels soft.

2. What feels hard?

   Rocks feel hard.

3. What feels cold?

   Ice feels cold.

4. What helps you to feel?

   My fingers help me to feel.

5. How many fingers do you have?

   I have ten fingers.

Page 10

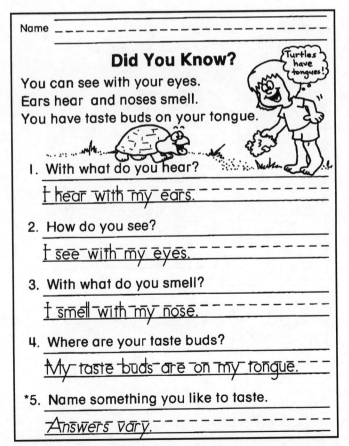

Name

Did You Know?

You can see with your eyes.
Ears hear and noses smell.
You have taste buds on your tongue.

1. With what do you hear?

   I hear with my ears.

2. How do you see?

   I see with my eyes.

3. With what do you smell?

   I smell with my nose.

4. Where are your taste buds?

   My taste buds are on my tongue.

*5. Name something you like to taste.

   Answers vary.

Page 11

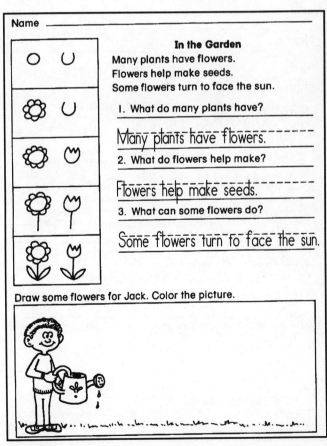

Name

In the Garden

Many plants have flowers.
Flowers help make seeds.
Some flowers turn to face the sun.

1. What do many plants have?

   Many plants have flowers.

2. What do flowers help make?

   Flowers help make seeds.

3. What can some flowers do?

   Some flowers turn to face the sun.

Draw some flowers for Jack. Color the picture.

Page 12

107

Answer Key

Name

Drip, Drip

Plants need water to grow.
The roots take up water from the soil.
The water goes up the stem to the leaves.

1. What do plants need?

   Plants need water.

2. How does the water get into the plant?

   The roots take up water.

3. Where are the plant's roots?

   The roots are in the soil.

4. How does the water get to the leaves?

   The water goes up the stem to the leaves

*5. What else do you think plants need?

   Answers vary.

Pet Care

A pet needs lots of love.
Feed it the kind of food that it needs.
Do you know that a pet can get sick
if it is bored?

1. What does a pet need?

   A pet needs lots of love.

2. What do we feed a pot?

   You feed it food that it needs.

3. What can happen to a bored pet?

   It can get sick.

*4. How can you find out what is the right food
   for your pet?

   Answers vary.

*5. What can you do with a dog so that it will not
   be bored?

   Answers vary.

Exotic Pets

Gasp!

It is very hard to keep wild animals.
They may need a big space to run around.
They may eat food that is hard
to get—like live spiders!

1. What is hard to do well?

   It is hard to keep wild animals.

2. What might wild animals need?

   They may need a big space to run around.

3. What might they need to eat?

   They may need to eat food that is hard to get.

*4. Do you have a zoo in your city?

   Answers vary.

*5. What are some things that a zoo keeper
   will need to know?

   Answers vary.

Sally Spider

A spider has eight legs.
A spider is not an insect.
Spiders eat insects!
Some spiders make webs.

1. How many legs do spiders have?

   Spiders have eight legs.

2. What do some spiders make?

   Some spiders make webs.

3. What do spiders eat?

   Spiders eat insects.

Draw spiders on the web.

108

Answer Key

Who Made the Holes?

Did you ever look at rocks at the seashore?
Some of the stones have holes in them.
Some clams make holes in soft stones.

1. Where can you find rocks with holes?

I can find rocks with holes at the seashore.

2. What can make holes in stones?

Some clams make holes in stones.

3. What is another word for **rock**?

Another word for rock is stone.

*4. Have you ever gone to the seashore?

Answers vary.

*5. Why do you think a clam makes holes in stones?

Answers vary.

Page 17

Time to Hibernate

In winter, some animals hide
and become **dormant**.
That means they are very still,
as if they were asleep.
My turtle stays in his hole
from November to March!

1. When do some animals hide?

Some animals hide in the winter.

2. What does **dormant** mean?

Dormant means very still.

3. When does my turtle hide in his hole?

Your turtle stays in his hole from November to March.

*4. What word means hide for the winter?

Hibernate means hide for the winter.

*5. Why do you think some animals hibernate?

Answers vary.

Page 18

Camouflage

Some animals use color to hide themselves.
A green bug is hard to see on a leaf.
Some rabbits turn white in winter
to match the snow.

1. How do some animals hide?

Some animals use color to hide themselves.

2. What is hard to see on a leaf?

A green bug is hard to see on a leaf.

3. What do some rabbits do in winter?

Some rabbits turn white in winter.

*4. What color is snow?

Snow is white.

*5. Where do you think a brown lizard can hide?

Answers vary.

Page 19

Nocturnal Animals

Some animals sleep in the daytime.
They come out at night to look for food.
Many desert animals like to come out at night.

1. What do some animals do in the daytime?

Some animals sleep in the daytime.

2. When do they come out?

They come out at night.

3. What do they do at night?

They look for food.

4. What kind of animals like to come out at night?

Desert animals like to come out at night.

*5. Why do many desert animals like to come out at night?

Answers vary.

Page 20

FS-32048 Science

Answer Key

Name _____

Newborns

Mama?

Some baby animals are born bald and blind.
They need their mothers for a long time.
Other babies are born with hair.
They are a lot like small adults.

1. Why do some babies need their mothers for a long time?

They are born bald and blind.

2. What are other babies like?

Other babies are like small adults.

3. What are some babies born with?

Some babies are born with hair.

*4. Find a word that means **can't see**.

Blind means can't see.

*5. Find a word that means **has no hair**.

Bald means has no hair.

Page 21

Name _____

Wild Animals

Some animals in the woods look so cute.
You may want to take them home with you.
I hope you will leave them free and happy
in the woods.

1. How do some wild animals look?

Some wild animals look cute.

2. What is it that you may want to do?

I may want to take them home.

3. What do I hope you will do?

You hope I will leave them free and happy.

*4. What can happen if you pick up a wild animal?

Answers vary.

*5. What wild animal looks cute to you?

Answers vary.

Page 22

Name _____

Rolling in the Mud

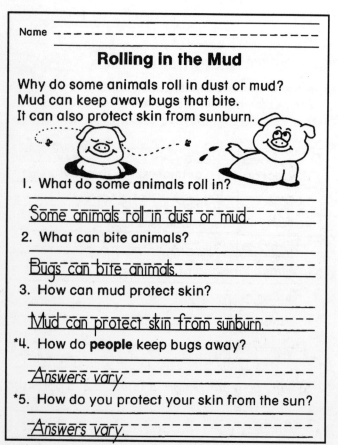

Why do some animals roll in dust or mud?
Mud can keep away bugs that bite.
It can also protect skin from sunburn.

1. What do some animals roll in?

Some animals roll in dust or mud.

2. What can bite animals?

Bugs can bite animals.

3. How can mud protect skin?

Mud can protect skin from sunburn.

*4. How do **people** keep bugs away?

Answers vary.

*5. How do you protect your skin from the sun?

Answers vary.

Page 23

Name _____

All Gone

Some animals are extinct.
That means there are none of them left now.
It is sad when an animal is the last of its kind.

1. What has happened to some kinds of animals?

Some animals are extinct.

2. What does extinct mean?

Extinct means there are none left now.

3. What is sad?

It is sad when an animal is the last of its kind.

*4. Do you think dinosaurs are extinct?

Yes, dinosaurs are extinct.

*5. Do you wish fleas were extinct?

Answers vary.

Page 24

110

FS-32048 Science

Answer Key

Mammals

Mammals have fur or hair.
Mammals have milk for their babies.
A person is a mammal, and so is a bunny.

1. What do mammals have for their babies?

Mammals have milk for their babies.

2. What else do mammals have?

Mammals have fur or hair.

3. Are you a mammal?

Yes, I am a mammal.

*4. Name a big mammal.

Answers vary.

*5. Name a tiny mammal.

Answers vary.

Page 25

Mammals in the Sea

Some mammals live in the sea.
A mother whale feeds milk to her baby.
Whales have to come up to breathe air.

1. Name a big sea mammal.

A whale is a big sea mammal.

2. What does a mother whale feed her baby?

A mother whale feeds her baby milk.

3. Why do whales come up?

Whales come up to breathe air.

*4. What kind of animal can breathe under water?

Fish can breathe under water.

*5. Do you think that a whale is a fish?

No, a whale is a mammal.

Page 26

Rodents

Squeak!

Rodents are a kind of mammal.
Rats, mice and beavers are rodents.
They have teeth that can chew very well!

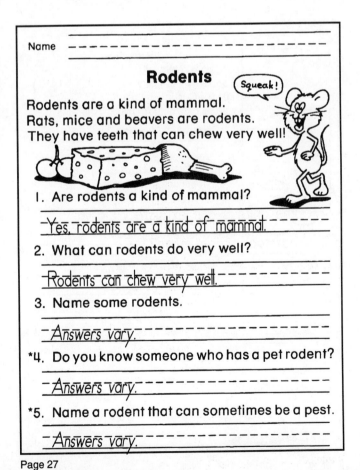

1. Are rodents a kind of mammal?

Yes, rodents are a kind of mammal.

2. What can rodents do very well?

Rodents can chew very well.

3. Name some rodents.

Answers vary.

*4. Do you know someone who has a pet rodent?

Answers vary.

*5. Name a rodent that can sometimes be a pest.

Answers vary.

Page 27

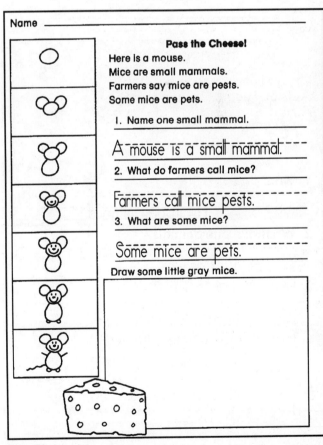

Pass the Cheese!

Here is a mouse.
Mice are small mammals.
Farmers say mice are pests.
Some mice are pets.

1. Name one small mammal.

A mouse is a small mammal.

2. What do farmers call mice?

Farmers call mice pests.

3. What are some mice?

Some mice are pets.

Draw some little gray mice.

Page 28

Answer Key

Name _____

The Elephant

The elephant is big and gray.
His nose is a long trunk.
He eats leaves from tree tops.

1. What is big?

The elephant is big.

2. What color is the elephant?

The elephant is gray.

3. What is long?

His trunk is long.

4. What do elephants eat?

Elephants eat leaves.

5. Where are the leaves?

The leaves are from tree tops.

Page 29

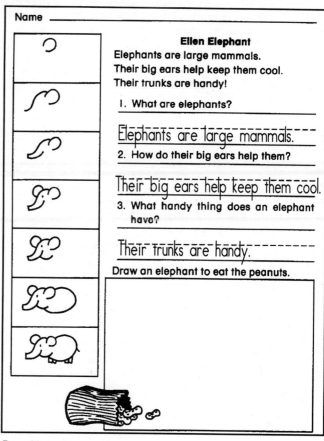

Name _____

Ellen Elephant
Elephants are large mammals.
Their big ears help keep them cool.
Their trunks are handy!

1. What are elephants?

Elephants are large mammals.

2. How do their big ears help them?

Their big ears help keep them cool.

3. What handy thing does an elephant have?

Their trunks are handy.

Draw an elephant to eat the peanuts.

Page 30

Name _____

Cats

Cats have four soft paws.
Cats keep their claws sharp.
They like to climb tall trees.

1. What are soft?

The paws are soft.

2. What are sharp?

The claws are sharp.

3. What can cats climb?

Cats can climb trees.

4. How many paws do cats have?

Cats have four paws.

5. What are tall?

The trees are tall.

Page 31

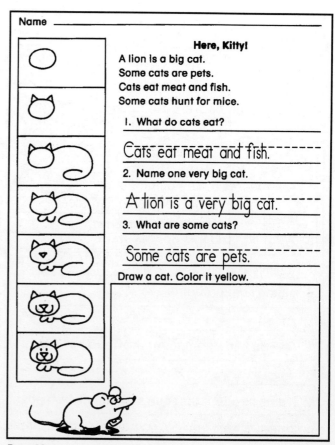

Name _____

Here, Kitty!
A lion is a big cat.
Some cats are pets.
Cats eat meat and fish.
Some cats hunt for mice.

1. What do cats eat?

Cats eat meat and fish.

2. Name one very big cat.

A lion is a very big cat.

3. What are some cats?

Some cats are pets.

Draw a cat. Color it yellow.

Page 32

Answer Key

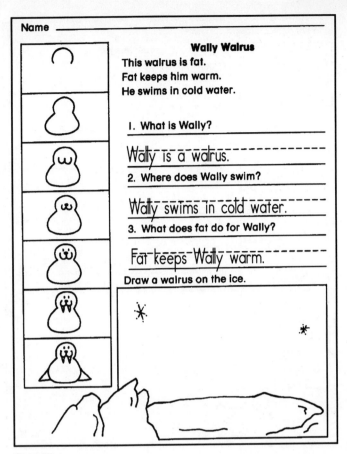

Wally Walrus

This walrus is fat.
Fat keeps him warm.
He swims in cold water.

1. What is Wally?

Wally is a walrus.

2. Where does Wally swim?

Wally swims in cold water.

3. What does fat do for Wally?

Fat keeps Wally warm.

Draw a walrus on the ice.

Page 33

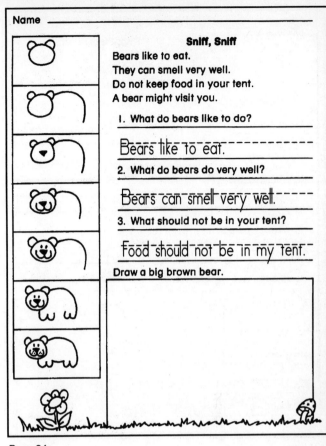

Sniff, Sniff

Bears like to eat.
They can smell very well.
Do not keep food in your tent.
A bear might visit you.

1. What do bears like to do?

Bears like to eat.

2. What do bears do very well?

Bears can smell very well.

3. What should not be in your tent?

Food should not be in my tent.

Draw a big brown bear.

Page 34

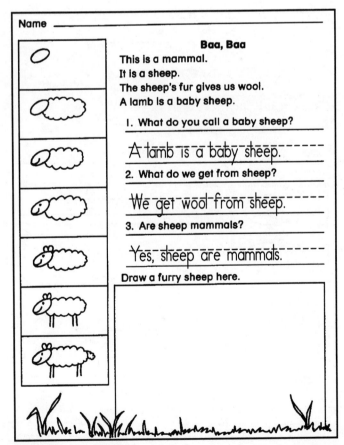

Baa, Baa

This is a mammal.
It is a sheep.
The sheep's fur gives us wool.
A lamb is a baby sheep.

1. What do you call a baby sheep?

A lamb is a baby sheep.

2. What do we get from sheep?

We get wool from sheep.

3. Are sheep mammals?

Yes, sheep are mammals.

Draw a furry sheep here.

Page 35

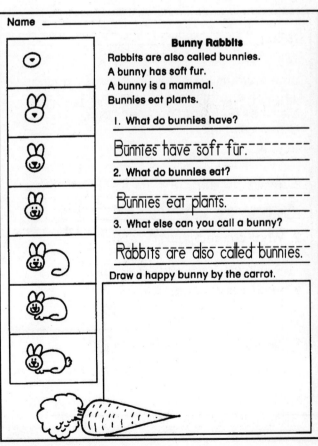

Bunny Rabbits

Rabbits are also called bunnies.
A bunny has soft fur.
A bunny is a mammal.
Bunnies eat plants.

1. What do bunnies have?

Bunnies have soft fur.

2. What do bunnies eat?

Bunnies eat plants.

3. What else can you call a bunny?

Rabbits are also called bunnies.

Draw a happy bunny by the carrot.

Page 36

113

Answer Key

Flap, Flap!

Bats can fly.
Bats are not birds.
Bats are like flying mice.
Some bats eat fruit.

1. What can bats do?

Bats can fly.

2. Are bats birds?

Bats are not birds.

3. What are bats like?

Bats are like flying mice.

Draw a bat in the night sky.

Page 37

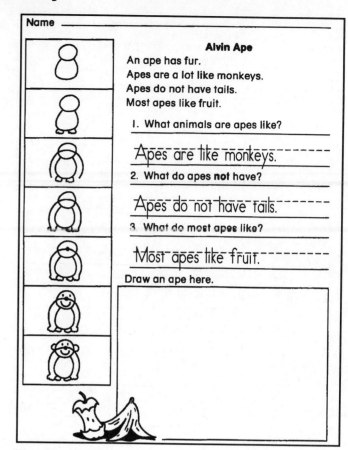

Alvin Ape

An ape has fur.
Apes are a lot like monkeys.
Apes do not have tails.
Most apes like fruit.

1. What animals are apes like?

Apes are like monkeys.

2. What do apes **not** have?

Apes do not have tails.

3. What do most apes like?

Most apes like fruit.

Draw an ape here.

Page 38

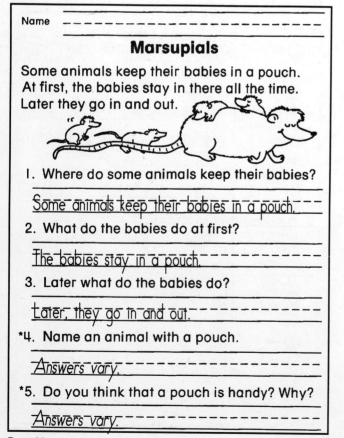

Marsupials

Some animals keep their babies in a pouch.
At first, the babies stay in there all the time.
Later they go in and out.

1. Where do some animals keep their babies?

Some animals keep their babies in a pouch.

2. What do the babies do at first?

The babies stay in a pouch.

3. Later what do the babies do?

Later, they go in and out.

*4. Name an animal with a pouch.

Answers vary.

*5. Do you think that a pouch is handy? Why?

Answers vary.

Page 39

Kangaroos

The gray kangaroo can hop fast.
She has strong back legs.
The baby is in her soft pocket.

1. What can hop fast?

The kangaroo can hop fast.

2. What are strong?

The back legs are strong.

3. What is soft?

Her pocket is soft.

4. Where is the baby?

The baby is in the pocket.

5. What color is the kangaroo?

The kangaroo is gray.

Page 40

114

FS-32048 Science

Answer Key

Name

Reptiles

A reptile has dry skin with scales.
A snake is one kind of reptile.
Dinosaurs were reptiles.

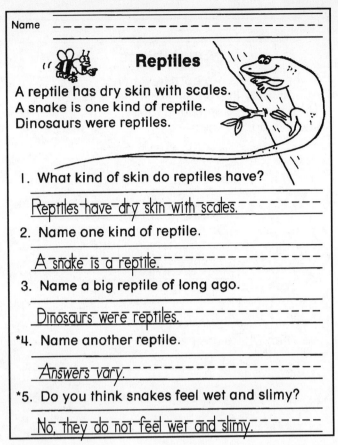

1. What kind of skin do reptiles have?

   Reptiles have dry skin with scales.

2. Name one kind of reptile.

   A snake is a reptile.

3. Name a big reptile of long ago.

   Dinosaurs were reptiles.

*4. Name another reptile.

   Answers vary.

*5. Do you think snakes feel wet and slimy?

   No, they do not feel wet and slimy.

Page 41

Name

Other Eggs

The little egg will soon hatch.
No bird will come out of it.
This egg is a turtle egg!

1. Is the egg big or little?

   The egg is little.

2. What will the egg soon do?

   The egg will soon hatch.

3. Will a bird come out?

   No, a bird will not come out.

4. Did a bird lay this egg?

   No, a bird did not lay this egg.

*5. What **will** come out?

   A turtle will come out.

Page 42

Name

Timmy Turtle

This turtle lives on land.
It does not have fur.
It has a hard shell.
Some turtles live in the water.

1. Where does this turtle live?

   This turtle lives on land.

2. Where do some turtles live?

   Some turtles live in water.

3. What does this turtle have?

   This turtle has a hard shell.

Draw a land turtle. Color the picture.

Page 43

Name

Baby Lizards

Some lizards are born alive.
Other kinds of lizards lay eggs.
Baby lizards are in those eggs.

1. Do all lizards lay eggs?

   No, all lizards do not lay eggs.

2. Do some lizards lay eggs?

   Yes, some lizards lay eggs.

*3. What other kinds of animals lay eggs?

   Answers vary.

4. What comes out of a lizard egg?

   A baby lizard comes out of the egg.

*5. Have you ever seen a bird egg?

   Answers vary.

Page 44

115

FS-32048 Science

Answer Key

Name _____

The Alligator

The alligator lives near water.
He has a long brown tail.
The tail helps him to swim.
He likes to eat fish.

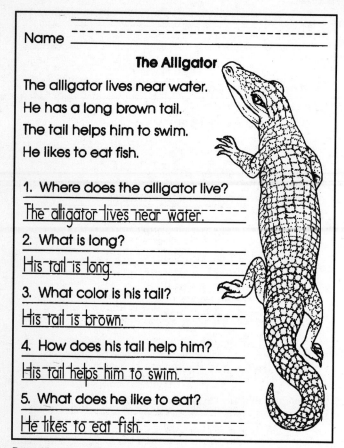

1. Where does the alligator live?

The alligator lives near water.

2. What is long?

His tail is long.

3. What color is his tail?

His tail is brown.

4. How does his tail help him?

His tail helps him to swim.

5. What does he like to eat?

He likes to eat fish.

Page 45

Name _____

Amphibians

Some animals are born in water.
At first, they live under water like a fish.
Then they grow legs and lungs,
and live out on land!

1. Where are amphibians born?

Amphibians are born in water.

2. What are they like at first?

At first they are like a fish.

3. Then what do they grow?

They grow legs and lungs.

4. Then where do they live?

They live on land.

*5. Have you ever seen a real live frog or toad?

Answers vary.

Page 46

Name _____

The Tadpole

The tadpole came from an egg.
Then it grew tiny legs.
The tadpole became a frog!

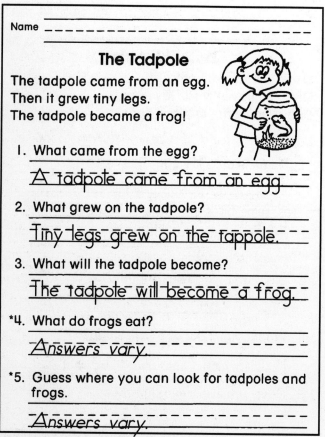

1. What came from the egg?

A tadpole came from an egg.

2. What grew on the tadpole?

Tiny legs grew on the tadpole.

3. What will the tadpole become?

The tadpole will become a frog.

*4. What do frogs eat?

Answers vary.

*5. Guess where you can look for tadpoles and frogs.

Answers vary.

Page 47

Name _____

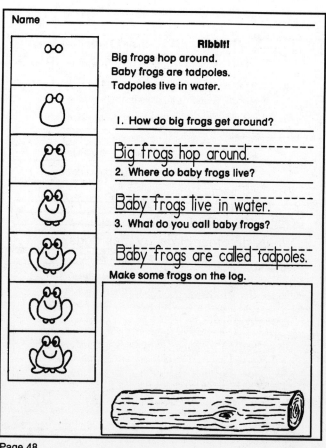

Ribbit!

Big frogs hop around.
Baby frogs are tadpoles.
Tadpoles live in water.

1. How do big frogs get around?

Big frogs hop around.

2. Where do baby frogs live?

Baby frogs live in water.

3. What do you call baby frogs?

Baby frogs are called tadpoles.

Make some frogs on the log.

Page 48

116

FS-32048 Science

Answer Key

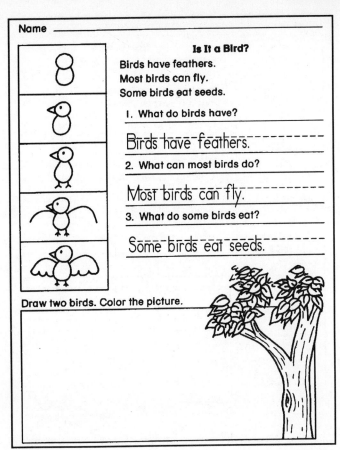

Name _____

Is It a Bird?
Birds have feathers.
Most birds can fly.
Some birds eat seeds.

1. What do birds have?

Birds have feathers.

2. What can most birds do?

Most birds can fly.

3. What do some birds eat?

Some birds eat seeds.

Draw two birds. Color the picture.

Page 49

Name _____

Birds

A bird has a beak and two legs.
Some birds can fly.
Bird eggs have hard shells.

1. What do birds have?

Birds have a beak and two legs.

2. What can some birds do?

Some birds can fly.

3. What has a hard shell?

Bird eggs have hard shells.

4. How many legs do birds have?

Birds have two legs.

*5. Is a butterfly a kind of bird?

No, a butterfly is not a bird.

Page 50

Name _____

Nesting Time

Some birds make a nest to hold their eggs.
Other birds lay their eggs right on the ground!
These eggs often look like rocks.
This helps to hide them.

1. What do some birds make?

Some birds make a nest.

2. Where do other birds lay their eggs?

Other birds lay their eggs on the ground.

3. What do these eggs often look like?

These eggs often look like rocks.

*4. Why do birds want to hide their eggs?

Answers vary.

*5. What do birds use to make nests?

Answers vary.

Page 51

Name _____

Some Birds Migrate

Some birds stay with us
even in the cold wintertime.
They have to look hard to find food.
Other birds fly away to lands that are warm.

1. Do some birds stay with us in winter?

Yes, some birds stay with us in winter.

2. What do other birds do?

Other birds fly away to lands that are warm.

3. Why do some birds fly away?

It is hard to find food or to get warm.

*4. Why is it hard to find food in winter?

Answers vary.

*5. Name some things that birds eat.

Answers vary.

Page 52

117

FS-32048 Science

Answer Key

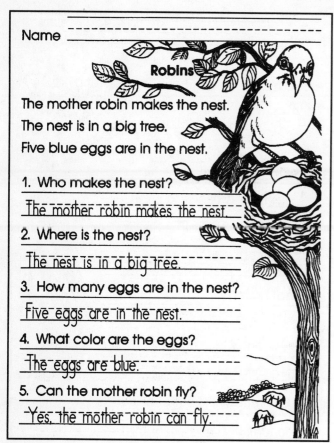

Name _____

Robins

The mother robin makes the nest.
The nest is in a big tree.
Five blue eggs are in the nest.

1. Who makes the nest?

The mother robin makes the nest.

2. Where is the nest?

The nest is in a big tree.

3. How many eggs are in the nest?

Five eggs are in the nest.

4. What color are the eggs?

The eggs are blue.

5. Can the mother robin fly?

Yes, the mother robin can fly.

Page 53

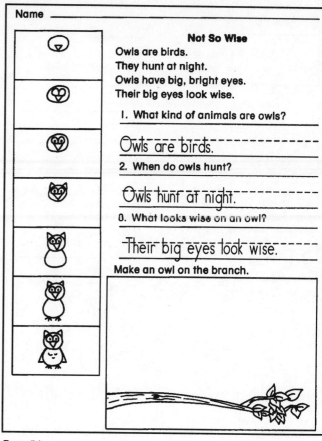

Name _____

Not So Wise

Owls are birds.
They hunt at night.
Owls have big, bright eyes.
Their big eyes look wise.

1. What kind of animals are owls?

Owls are birds.

2. When do owls hunt?

Owls hunt at night.

0. What looks wise on an owl?

Their big eyes look wise.

Make an owl on the branch.

Page 54

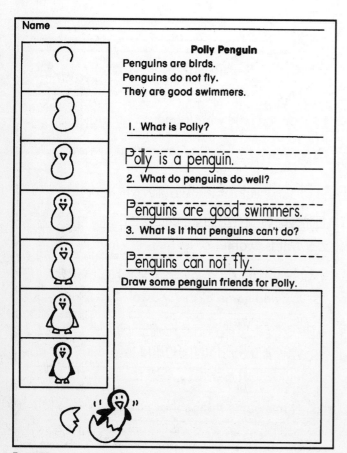

Name _____

Polly Penguin

Penguins are birds.
Penguins do not fly.
They are good swimmers.

1. What is Polly?

Polly is a penguin.

2. What do penguins do well?

Penguins are good swimmers.

3. What is it that penguins can't do?

Penguins can not fly.

Draw some penguin friends for Polly.

Page 55

Name _____

Fish

Fish have scales.
They can breathe under water.
Some fish live in salt water.

1. What do fish have?

Fish have scales.

2. Where can fish breathe?

Fish can breathe under water.

3. Where do some fish live?

Some fish live in salt water.

*4. Do fish have fur?

No, fish do not have fur.

*5. Do fish have legs?

No, fish do not have legs.

Page 56

118

FS-32048 Science

Answer Key

Name _____

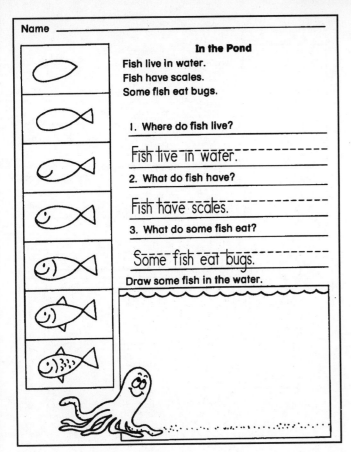

In the Pond

Fish live in water.
Fish have scales.
Some fish eat bugs.

1. Where do fish live?

Fish live in water.

2. What do fish have?

Fish have scales.

3. What do some fish eat?

Some fish eat bugs.

Draw some fish in the water.

Page 57

Name _____

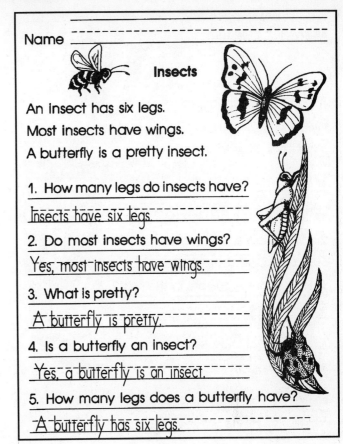

Insects

An insect has six legs.
Most insects have wings.
A butterfly is a pretty insect.

1. How many legs do insects have?

Insects have six legs.

2. Do most insects have wings?

Yes, most insects have wings.

3. What is pretty?

A butterfly is pretty.

4. Is a butterfly an insect?

Yes, a butterfly is an insect.

5. How many legs does a butterfly have?

A butterfly has six legs.

Page 58

Name _____

Grasshoppers

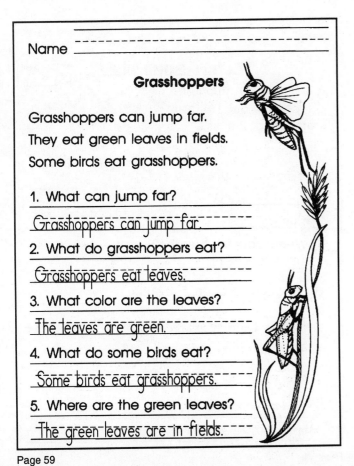

Grasshoppers can jump far.
They eat green leaves in fields.
Some birds eat grasshoppers.

1. What can jump far?

Grasshoppers can jump far.

2. What do grasshoppers eat?

Grasshoppers eat leaves.

3. What color are the leaves?

The leaves are green.

4. What do some birds eat?

Some birds eat grasshoppers.

5. Where are the green leaves?

The green leaves are in fields.

Page 59

Name _____

Honeybees

Honeybees are helpful insects.
They make sweet honey and wax.
Bees help flowers become fruit.

1. Which insects are helpful?

Honeybees are helpful insects.

2. What is sweet?

Honey is sweet.

3. What makes wax?

Honeybees make wax.

4. What do flowers become?

Flowers become fruit.

5. Are honeybees insects?

Yes, honeybees are insects.

Page 60

119

FS-32048 Science

Answer Key

Name

Crickets

A cricket is a jumping insect.
Some crickets go into houses.
Crickets rub their wings to sing.

1. What is a cricket?

A cricket is a jumping insect.

2. Where do some crickets go?

Some crickets go into houses.

3. How do crickets sing?

Crickets rub their wings to sing.

4. Do crickets jump?

Yes, crickets can jump.

5. Could you have a cricket in your house?

Yes, I could have a cricket in my house.

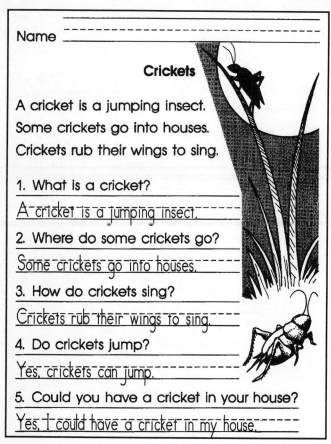

Page 61

Name

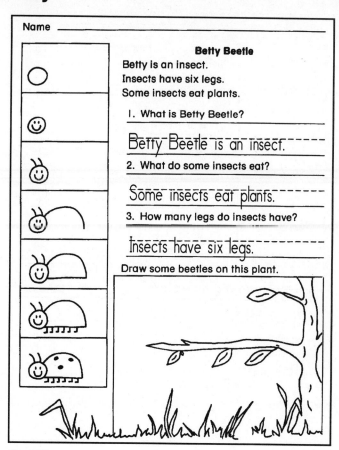

Betty Beetle

Betty is an insect.
Insects have six legs.
Some insects eat plants.

1. What is Betty Beetle?

Betty Beetle is an insect.

2. What do some insects eat?

Some insects eat plants.

3. How many legs do insects have?

Insects have six legs.

Draw some beetles on this plant.

Page 62

Name

Caterpillars

Caterpillars are baby butterflies.
The caterpillars eat plants.
They make a cocoon.
Then the adult butterfly comes out!

1. What are baby butterflies?

Caterpillars are baby butterflies.

2. What do they eat?

They eat plants.

3. What do they make?

They make a cocoon.

Draw a butterfly. Color the picture.

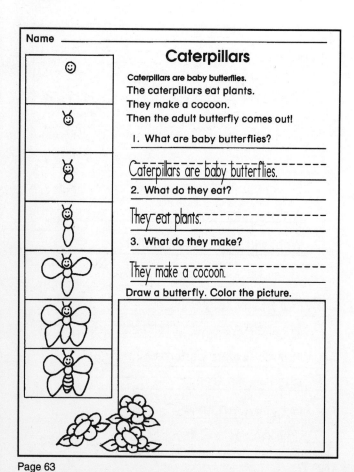

Page 63

Name

Before Butterflies

A tiny egg lay on a leaf.
Out came a caterpillar!
It ate lots of leaves.

1. Where was the egg?

The egg was on a leaf.

2. Was the egg big or tiny?

The egg was tiny.

3. What came out of the egg?

A caterpillar came out of the egg.

4. What did the caterpillar eat?

The caterpillar ate leaves.

*5. Guess what the caterpillar will become.

Answers vary.

Page 64

120

FS-32048 Science

Answer Key

Name _____

Surprise

The caterpillar turned into a pupa.
It lay very still for many weeks.
Then out came a butterfly.

1. What turned into a pupa?

   The caterpillar turned into a pupa.

2. Did the pupa move around?

   No, it did not.

3. How long did it lie still?

   It lay still for many weeks.

4. What came out of the pupa?

   A butterfly came out of the pupa.

*5. Have you ever seen a caterpillar?

   Answers vary.

Name _____

The Moth

Some caterpillars do not become butterflies.
Many of them become moths.
A moth is a lot like a butterfly.

1. Do all caterpillars become butterflies?

   No, all caterpillars do not become butterflies.

2. What is like a butterfly?

   A moth is like a butterfly.

3. Name two things a caterpillar may become.

   A caterpillar may become a moth or a butterfly.

*4. Were you once a caterpillar?

   No, I was not a caterpillar.

*5. How is a moth like a butterfly?

   Answer vary.

Name _____

Pests

Many caterpillars are **pests**.
They will eat buds and leaves.
They may make holes in your fruit!

1. What do we call caterpillars who are a bother?

   Caterpillars who are a bother are called pests.

2. What will they eat?

   They will eat buds and leaves.

3. What do they do to fruit?

   They make holes in fruit.

*4. Can you name another pest?

   Answers vary.

*5. What do you think **pest** means?

   Answers vary.

Name _____

Inside an Apple

You may find a caterpillar in your apple.
Most people will call it a worm.
A caterpillar is a little like a worm.

1. Where can you find a caterpillar?

   A caterpillar can be found in an apple.

2. What will some people call it?

   Some people will call it a worm.

3. What is like a caterpillar?

   A worm is like a caterpillar.

*4. How are caterpillars and worms alike?

   Answers vary.

*5. Did you ever find a bug in your food?

   Answers vary.

Answer Key

Name

Will It Float?

Fill a pail with water.
Drop little things in the water.
Make a chart to show what floats.

1. Where will you put the water?

   I will put the water in a pail.

2. What goes into the water?

   Little things go into the water.

3. Then what will you make?

   I will make a chart.

4. What will it show?

   The chart will show what floats.

*5. Name something you think will sink.

   Answers vary.

Page 69

Name

Like Magic

Your teacher may have a magnet.
A magnet will not stick to wood or paper.
It will stick to some kinds of metal.

1. Who may have a magnet?

   My teacher may have a magnet.

2. What does not stick to a magnet?

   Wood or paper will not stick to a magnet.

3. What may stick to a magnet?

   Some metal will stick to a magnet.

*4. Is there a magnet in your class?

   Answers vary.

*5. Name some little things you think will stick to a magnet.

   Answers vary.

Page 70

Name

When You Play . . .

It is a good idea to have a friend with you.
If you get hurt, your pal can get help.
You are safer if you are not alone.

1. What is a good idea?

   It is a good idea to have a friend with me.

2. What can your pal do?

   My pal can get help.

3. When can your pal get help?

   My pal can get help if I get hurt.

4. When are you safer?

   I am safer if I am not alone.

*5. Name a pal you like to play with.

   Answers vary.

Page 71

Name

Eat Healthy Foods

You need to eat good food each day.
Some good foods are milk, meat and fruit.
Don't eat too much junk food!

1. What do you need to eat each day?

   I need to eat good food.

2. Name some good foods.

   Milk, meat and fruit are good foods.

*3. Name a fruit you like.

   Answers vary.

*4. Name some junk foods.

   Answers vary.

*5. How does good food help you?

   Answers vary.

Page 72

Answer Key

Clean Hands

Wash your hands before you eat.
Did you know little germs live there?
They are tiny, but they are real!

SOAP

1. When should you wash your hands?

   I should wash my hands before I eat.

2. What may be on your hands?

   Little germs could be on my hands.

3. What are tiny?

   Germs are tiny.

4. Are germs real?

   Yes, germs are real.

*5. Why do we want to wash germs off?

   Answers vary.

Page 73

Don't Sneeze on Me!

Cover your sneeze.
You can turn away, too.
Nobody wants to get your germs.

1. What do you cover?

   I cover my sneeze.

2. What else can you do?

   I can turn away.

3. What is it nobody wants to get?

   Nobody wants to get my germs.

*4. Why not?

   Answers vary.

*5. Did you ever have a cold?

   Answers vary.

Page 74

Taking Medicine

If you're sick, Mom may give you a pill.
Do not take a pill unless Mom
or Dad gives it to you.
You can become very sick if you do!

1. What can make you very sick?

   A pill can make me very sick.

2. When might Mom give you a pill?

   Mom might give me a pill when I am sick.

*3. Should you give yourself pills?

   No, I should not give myself pills.

*4. Do you take pills from other kids?

   No, I do not take pills from other kids.

*5. Did you ever feel sick?

   Answers vary.

Page 75

Be Kind to Animals

Do not tease any pets.
They have feelings, too!
Pets may scratch or bite if you scare them.

FIDO

1. What do we never do to pets?

   Never tease any pets.

2. Why is it mean to tease pets?

   They have feelings, too.

3. What might scared pets do to you?

   Scared pets might scratch or bite.

*4. What kind of pet do you like?

   Answers vary.

*5. Do you like people to tease you?

   Answers vary.

Page 76

FS-32048 Science

Answer Key

Name _____

Clean Up!

Put your toys away after you play.
Toys on the floor can trip people.
You may lose toys if you don't put them away.

1. What do you do after you play with toys?

   I put my toys away after I play.

2. What can trip people?

   Toys on the floor can trip people.

3. What can happen to toys if you don't put them away?

   I may lose toys.

*4. Where do you keep your toys?

   Answers vary.

*5. Did you ever lose a toy?

   Answers vary.

Page 77

Name _____

In the Car

Do not bother Mom when she is driving.
Stay in your seat belt and face the front.
If you fight or yell, Mom may crash!

1. Where do you stay when Mom is driving?

   I stay in my seat belt.

2. Where do you face?

   I face the front.

3. If you fight, what may happen?

   Mom may crash.

*4. Can Mom look at you and drive too?

   No, Mom can not look at me and drive too.

*5. Can you put on your own seat belt?

   Answers vary.

Page 78

Name _____

Cross Carefully

Look both ways before you cross the street.
Try to cross at a corner or in a crosswalk.
If there is a light, wait for the green light.

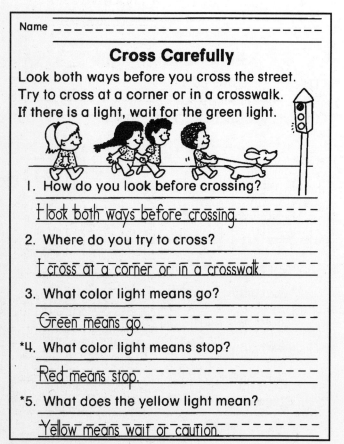

1. How do you look before crossing?

   I look both ways before crossing.

2. Where do you try to cross?

   I cross at a corner or in a crosswalk.

3. What color light means go?

   Green means go.

*4. What color light means stop?

   Red means stop.

*5. What does the yellow light mean?

   Yellow means wait or caution.

Page 79

Name _____

Telephone Safety

Do you know how to use the telephone?
The telephone is not a toy.
Have someone show you how to call for help.

1. Is the telephone a toy?

   No, the telephone is not a toy.

*2. Who can show you how to call on the telephone?

   Answers vary.

*3. What is your telephone number?

   Answers vary.

*4. What number can you call for help?

   Answers vary.

*5. Does your telephone have a dial, or buttons?

   Answers vary.

Page 80

124

FS-32048 Science

Answer Key

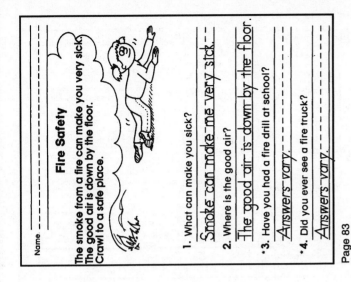

Fire Safety

Name _____

The smoke from a fire can make you very sick. The good air is down by the floor. Crawl to a safe place.

1. What can make you sick?
   Smoke can make me very sick.

2. Where is the good air?
   The good air is down by the floor.

*3. Have you had a fire drill at school?
   Answers vary.

*4. Did you ever see a fire truck?
   Answers vary.

Page 83

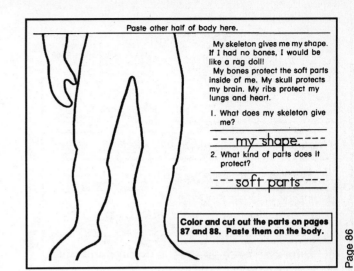

Paste other half of body here.

My skeleton gives me my shape. If I had no bones, I would be like a rag doll!
My bones protect the soft parts inside of me. My skull protects my brain. My ribs protect my lungs and heart.

1. What does my skeleton give me?
   my shape.

2. What kind of parts does it protect?
   soft parts

Color and cut out the parts on pages 87 and 88. Paste them on the body.

Page 86

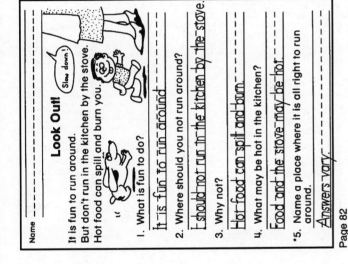

Look Out!

Name _____

(Slow down!)

It is fun to run around. But don't run in the kitchen by the stove. Hot food can spill and burn you.

1. What is fun to do?
   It is fun to run around

2. Where should you not run around?
   I should not run in the kitchen by the stove.

3. Why not?
   Hot food can spill and burn.

4. What may be hot in the kitchen?
   Food and the stove may be hot

*5. Name a place where it is all right to run around.
   Answers vary.

Page 82

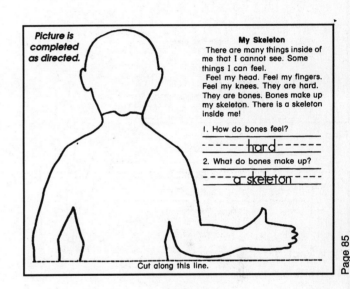

Picture is completed as directed.

My Skeleton

There are many things inside of me that I cannot see. Some things I can feel.
Feel my head. Feel my fingers. Feel my knees. They are hard. They are bones. Bones make up my skeleton. There is a skeleton inside me!

1. How do bones feel?
   hard

2. What do bones make up?
   a skeleton

Cut along this line.

Page 85

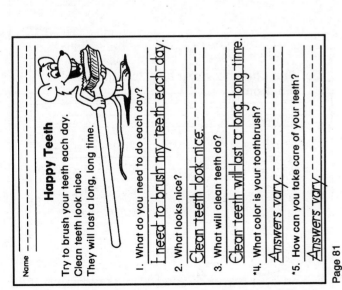

Happy Teeth

Name _____

Try to brush your teeth each day. Clean teeth look nice. They will last a long, long time.

1. What do you need to do each day?
   I need to brush my teeth each day.

2. What looks nice?
   Clean teeth look nice.

3. What will clean teeth do?
   Clean teeth will last a long, long time.

*4. What color is your toothbrush?
   Answers vary.

*5. How can you take care of your teeth?
   Answers vary.

Page 81

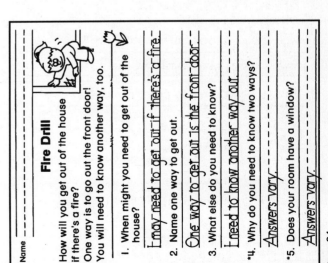

Fire Drill

Name _____

How will you get out of the house if there's a fire? One way is to go out the front door! You will need to know another way, too.

1. When might you need to get out of the house?
   I may need to get out if there's a fire.

2. Name one way to get out.
   One way to get out is the front door.

3. What else do you need to know?
   I need to know another way out

*4. Why do you need to know two ways?
   Answers vary.

*5. Does your room have a window?
   Answers vary.

Page 84

125

FS-32048 Science

Answer Key

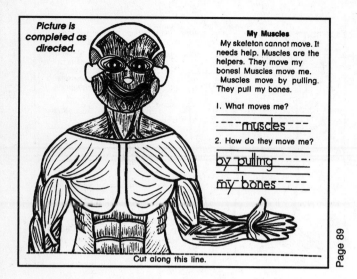

Picture is completed as directed.

My Muscles
My skeleton cannot move. It needs help. Muscles are the helpers. They move my bones! Muscles move me. Muscles move by pulling. They pull my bones.

1. What moves me?

muscles

2. How do they move me?

by pulling my bones

Cut along this line.

Page 89

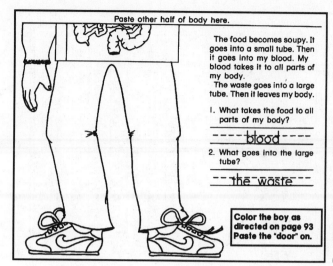

Paste other half of body here.

The food becomes soupy. It goes into a small tube. Then it goes into my blood. My blood takes it to all parts of my body.
The waste goes into a large tube. Then it leaves my body.

1. What takes the food to all parts of my body?

blood

2. What goes into the large tube?

the waste

Color the boy as directed on page 93. Paste the "door" on.

Page 92

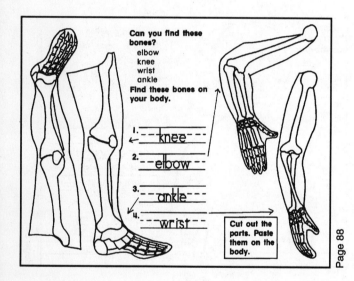

Can you find these bones?
elbow
knee
wrist
ankle

Find these bones on your body.

1. knee
2. elbow
3. ankle
4. wrist

Cut out the parts. Paste them on the body.

Page 88

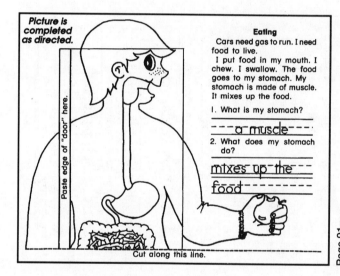

Picture is completed as directed.

Paste edge of "door" here.

Eating
Cars need gas to run. I need food to live.
I put food in my mouth. I chew. I swallow. The food goes to my stomach. My stomach is made of muscle. It mixes up the food.

1. What is my stomach?

a muscle

2. What does my stomach do?

mixes up the food

Cut along this line.

Page 91

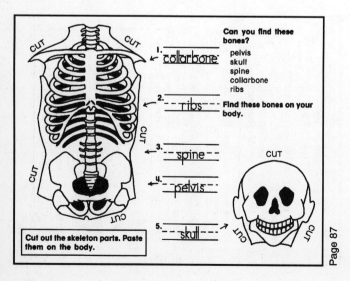

CUT   CUT

CUT

CUT

CUT

Can you find these bones?
pelvis
skull
spine
collarbone
ribs

Find these bones on your body.

1. collarbone
2. ribs
3. spine
4. pelvis
5. skull

CUT

CUT   CUT

Cut out the skeleton parts. Paste them on the body.

Page 87

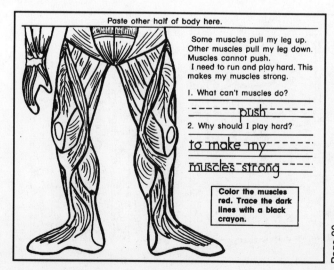

Paste other half of body here.

Some muscles pull my leg up. Other muscles pull my leg down. Muscles cannot push.
I need to run and play hard. This makes my muscles strong.

1. What can't muscles do?

push

2. Why should I play hard?

to make my muscles strong

Color the muscles red. Trace the dark lines with a black crayon.

Page 90

126

FS-32048 Science

Answer Key

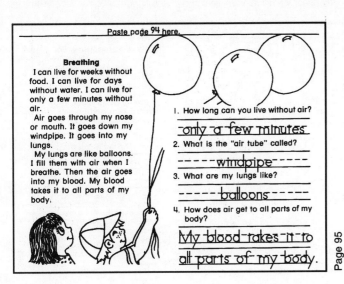

Breathing

I can live for weeks without food. I can live for days without water. I can live for only a few minutes without air.

Air goes through my nose or mouth. It goes down my windpipe. It goes into my lungs.

My lungs are like balloons. I fill them with air when I breathe. Then the air goes into my blood. My blood takes it to all parts of my body.

Paste page 94 here.

1. How long can you live without air?

<u>only a few minutes</u>

2. What is the "air tube" called?

<u>windpipe</u>

3. What are my lungs like?

<u>balloons</u>

4. How does air get to all parts of my body?

<u>My blood takes it to all parts of my body.</u>

Page 95

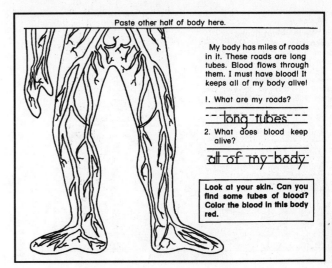

Paste other half of body here.

My body has miles of roads in it. These roads are long tubes. Blood flows through them. I must have blood! It keeps all of my body alive!

1. What are my roads?

<u>long tubes</u>

2. What does blood keep alive?

<u>all of my body</u>

Look at your skin. Can you find some tubes of blood? Color the blood in this body red.

Page 98

Picture is completed as directed.

Paste edge of "door" here.

My Lungs

<u>nostril</u>

<u>mouth</u>

<u>windpipe</u>

<u>lungs</u>

<u>heart</u>

Color the girl as directed on page 96. Paste the "door" on. Trace the words. Draw lines from the words to the correct body parts.

Cut along this line.

Page 94

Picture is completed as directed.

My Blood

My body needs food. My body needs air. Every part needs both food and air. How does food go from my stomach to my ear? How does air go from my lungs to my toes? My blood takes them!

lungs

heart

1. What does my body need?

<u>food and air</u>

2. What takes them?

<u>my blood</u>

Cut along this line.

Page 97

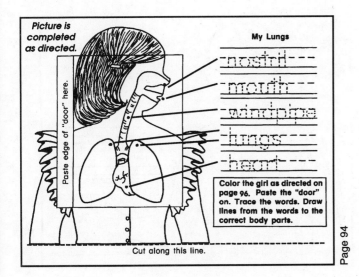

Color the boy and cut out the "door". Paste it on pages 91 and 92.

Cut   Cut

Picture is pasted on pages 91 and 92.

Cut   Cut

Color the body parts on **pages 91 and 92** as shown below.

mouth: red

food tube: yellow →

stomach: red

small tube: yellow

large tube: light red

Page 93

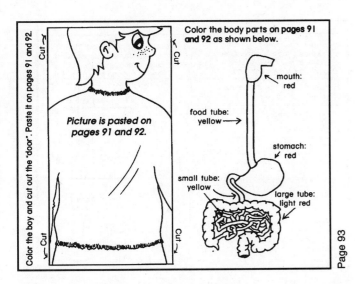

Color the girl and cut out the "door." Paste it on page 94.

cut

cut

Picture is pasted on page 94.

cut

cut

Color the body parts **on page 94.**

nostril: light red →

mouth: red

windpipe: yellow →

lung: light red

lung: light red

heart: red

SAFETY TIP!

The windpipe has a little door over it. This is to make sure that when you swallow, food will not go into the windpipe. Sometimes you gulp air when you eat. Then the door opens. Food goes in and you choke. Someone must squeeze you hard and fast just below your ribs. This makes air come up. The door opens and out pops the food!

Page 96

FS-32048 Science

Answer Key

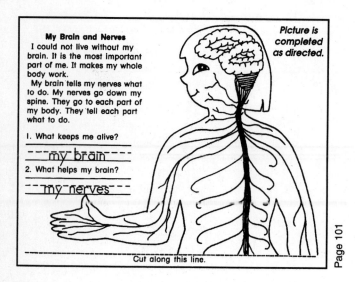

My Brain and Nerves

I could not live without my brain. It is the most important part of me. It makes my whole body work.

My brain tells my nerves what to do. My nerves go down my spine. They go to each part of my body. They tell each part what to do.

I. What keeps me alive?

my brain

2. What helps my brain?

my nerves

Picture is completed as directed.

Cut along this line.

Page 101

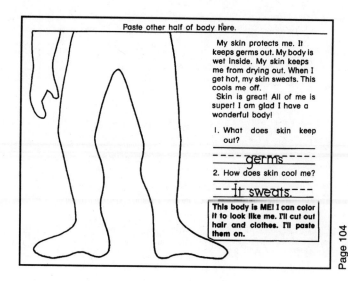

Paste other half of body here.

My skin protects me. It keeps germs out. My body is wet inside. My skin keeps me from drying out. When I get hot, my skin sweats. This cools me off.

Skin is great! All of me is super! I am glad I have a wonderful body!

I. What does skin keep out?

germs

2. How does skin cool me?

It sweats.

This body is ME! I can color it to look like me. I'll cut out hair and clothes. I'll paste them on.

Page 104

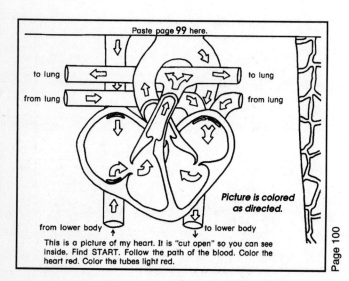

Paste page 99 here.

to lung

from lung

to lung

from lung

from lower body

to lower body

This is a picture of my heart. It is "cut open" so you can see inside. Find START. Follow the path of the blood. Color the heart red. Color the tubes light red.

Picture is colored as directed.

Page 100

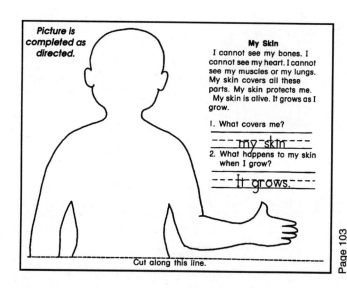

Picture is completed as directed.

My Skin

I cannot see my bones. I cannot see my heart. I cannot see my muscles or my lungs. My skin covers all these parts. My skin protects me. My skin is alive. It grows as I grow.

I. What covers me?

my skin

2. What happens to my skin when I grow?

It grows.

Cut along this line.

Page 103

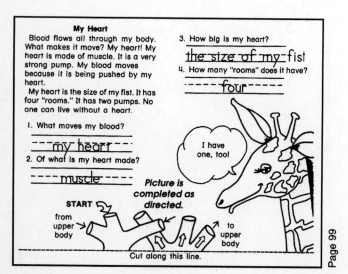

My Heart

Blood flows all through my body. What makes it move? My heart! My heart is made of muscle. It is a very strong pump. My blood moves because it is being pushed by my heart.

My heart is the size of my fist. It has four "rooms." It has two pumps. No one can live without a heart.

I. What moves my blood?

my heart

2. Of what is my heart made?

muscle

3. How big is my heart?

the size of my fist

4. How many "rooms" does it have?

four

I have one, too!

Picture is completed as directed.

START

from upper body

to upper body

Cut along this line.

Page 99

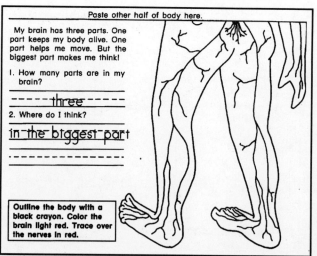

Paste other half of body here.

My brain has three parts. One part keeps my body alive. One part helps me move. But the biggest part makes me think!

I. How many parts are in my brain?

three

2. Where do I think?

in the biggest part

Outline the body with a black crayon. Color the brain light red. Trace over the nerves in red.

Page 102

128